Elizabeth R. Skoglund

A Cup of Coffee with God

Insights Along the Way

A Cup of Coffee with God
© 2019 by Elizabeth R. Skoglund.
Published by Netmenders.
All rights reserved.

Cover design by John Whorrall Jr.

ISBN: 978-0-578-60926-3

Library of Congress Control Number: 2019918397

Scripture quotations, unless otherwise indicated, are taken from *The Holy Bible, Authorized (King James) Version*.

Printed in the United States of America.

To My Aunt Ruth Caroline Benson

My Aunt Ruth spent her life as a missionary to the Chinese. When I was four or five, she was on furlough from China and later she was ministering to the Chinese in the United States. At those times she not only taught me Chinese cooking and customs but, above all, she showed me what it means to give one's whole life to God's service.

When she was 24, she applied to the China Inland Mission, which at that time was under the directorship of D.E. Hoste, who followed James Hudson Taylor, its founder. She described her work in the northern part of China as being primarily with women and children.

Years later she spent time in what was then called Formosa, now called Taiwan. Following that period of endeavor, she opened up a small mission for the Chinese in Los Angeles, California.

All of this occurred before I was born and then during my growing up years and early adulthood. She never really retired from her passion and love for the Chinese.

Betty M. Hu, Vice President of Bethel Mission of China, was a close friend of mine and told me that she had never known anyone but my aunt to learn Mandarin after childhood and still speak without a foreign accent. She was definitely a role model in many ways.

And the Lord spake unto Moses face to face, as a man speaketh unto his friend. (Exodus 33:11)

Henceforth I call you not servants; for the servant knoweth not what his lord doeth: but I have called you friends … (John 15:15)

Contents

Acknowledgments

Vital to the publication of several of my books has been the collective skills and efforts of John Whorrall Jr. and Lance Wilcox. John's creative skills are amazing, as seen in his production of the cover of *A Cup of Coffee with God*. Without the electronic skill and literary background of Lance, the book would not have been put together into such a perfect format. Both men gave freely of their time and skill.

Rayne Wilcox and Elizabeth Hannah Wilcox were a constant help in so-called "small things" which ended up being vital. In addition, Rayne provided special help in researching biblical areas like translations of certain words and finding occasional Bible passages.

Underlying all of these is my deep appreciation for the prayers of many, like Netmenders, a prayer group which meets monthly in my home, along with the wonderful example and teaching of lifetime mentors from the past like Alfred Crick, Drs. Marchant and Grace King, Dr. Pamela Reeve, Beverly West, various churches like the Church of the Open Door, the First Presbyterian Church of Hollywood and University Bible Church.

More currently, I am thankful for Father Jose Poch and those at St. David's Anglican Church in Burbank for their prayer support and for Father Jose's teaching and example in areas like prayer and Bible study.

A Cup of Coffee with God takes a somewhat autobiographical approach. My prayer is that it will encourage others to walk with reverent familiarity with our Lord Jesus Christ.

Foreword

It is interesting to see how God uses apparent misfortune to develop a much more fruitful ministry. Left to his own devices, St. Paul would have rampaged throughout the entire known world spreading the Gospel. Yet stuck in a series of fetid Roman prisons, he was forced to write letters to churches which he had planted years before, and those letters formed the bulk of New Testament Scriptures which have nurtured the ever-growing Christian church for more than two thousand years. Similarly, if John Bunyan had not been locked up in Bedford prison because of his faith, the world would never have seen that most widely read Christian classic – *Pilgrim's Progress*.

And so it is with *A Cup of Coffee with God*. On the surface, this unconventional book by Elizabeth Skoglund reads like an autobiography, moving back and forth from childhood to adolescence, to various phases of adulthood and back to her youth until she reaches her final destiny – a sort of Christian *vade mecum*, from which it becomes clear that the written word of God, implanted in her as a child by her elders, and, as she grew, from her own reading, was central to making her the spiritually powerful person that she has become. She neither evades nor conceals "the slings and arrows of outrageous fortune," confronting the pain caused by the death of loved ones and the sadness of having to surrender the love of her life because he was not willing to follow Jesus with her. Most long-lasting of all was the abrupt and persistent intrusion of Chronic Fatigue Syndrome, which cut across her long-held ambitions to found an orphanage or to serve as a missionary in China. Being confined not by iron bars but by physical illness, Ms. Skoglund declares that this very illness "was not some giant mistake God made in an off moment. Rather He used it to make me into someone who would understand and help people. He didn't want me to start a school or orphanage. But He did want me to teach and then to write and do psychotherapy."

Emerging from this richly woven tapestry of a life well lived is the sweetest finding of all: **God wants to be our friend**. Can you imagine? Sitting down with the Almighty, the Creator of the Universe, sharing a deep conversation over a cup of Fair Trade coffee? Preposterous – but yet it's not. From the time of the disaster in the Garden of Eden, God has made it clear that He desires to restore a close personal relationship with mankind. In the desert He set up his tabernacle with the Israelites. Through Hosea we can hear the anguish in God's voice as He deals with His wayward people who persistently stray from Him. He cries out "How can I give you up, O Israel? … For I am God and not man, the Holy One in your midst." His final plea, His last and best offer, has been to send us His Son, so much does He long to be our friend.

With whom else would you sit down and share such deep conversation and a cup of coffee? So often we engage in what one preacher called "a drive-by quiet time," presenting God with a to-do list for Him to deal with while we rush on to our next appointment. "Wait," cries God, "I want to spend *time* with you!" Such a conversation does not involve the spoken word so much as meditation and thoughts inspired by God from His written word if, and it's a big *if*, we have taken the time to "read, mark, learn and inwardly digest" the Word of God. Throughout this fascinating journey through her life, we see how richly she was blessed by the spiritual wealth of her parents and other older relatives. "Bring up a child in the way that (s)he shall go, and when (s)he is old, (s)he will not depart from it."

During times of misfortune, God patiently guides the affected person away from what they cannot do to things they can do in ever greater measure. Church history is replete with examples of people who, though weak in the eyes of the world, became mighty warriors, especially in prayer.

The mystery of prayer is that it works at all. An omnipotent God clearly does not need us, but yet He has ordained that without our prayers, He will not act. As Pascal said, "God instituted prayer in order to lend His creatures the dignity of causality." Spurgeon viewed prayer as "the slender nerve that moves the muscles of omnipotence."

Ms Skoglund, more than many of us, has developed the practice of intimate prayer (with coffee!) and explores what it means to pray "in Jesus' name" (for some, simply a mindless phrase added to the end of the "shopping list" to which they want God to attend). Jesus certainly promised that when we pray "in His name", this becomes a prayer that God accepts, but it surely does not allow us to ask things of God which by His very nature He would not do. Rather, when His Spirit is within us and motivates our prayer, our transformed nature could only ask of the Father what His will is to provide. "In My name" becomes a wellspring of power in prayer. Ms. Skoglund writes, "Since I became more aware of the power in that name, I began to feel a new strength as I prayed, and an awe of that precious name, and a worship of the One to whom it belongs, Jesus of Nazareth."

Towards the end of this book, Ms. Skoglund speaks of that time when our earthly life draws to a close. Many dread the doctor visits and the pronouncement of a terminal diagnosis. But yet, though the walk through the valley of the shadow of death may be painful, for most at the last there is rarely pain and anguish. Rather, it is a gentle process of casting off life's moorings, in the course of which many proclaim (as Ms. Skoglund's book describes) that they can see loved ones that they lost long ago, and gladly and peacefully they cross over to the other side. There might even be a pot of coffee waiting on the stove!

The arc of Ms. Skoglund's life is well described by the words of Thomas Cranmer, one-time Archbishop of Canterbury: "Oh God, you have put our feet on paths we do not wish to follow; you have led us down roads on which we do not wish to travel; in order to bring us to a place we would never want to leave." So may it be for those who draw inspiration from this unusual book.

– Matthew E. Conolly, M.D.
Professor Emeritus
David Geffen School of Medicine at UCLA

ONE

A Century of Change

Sunday was an excursion into the past. After some sporadic attempts at genealogy, I had decided that I simply didn't have the time, and so I had stopped my subscription to the genealogy website which I was using. In the few days I had remaining on my subscription, I felt I should give it one further try. Sunday afternoon gave me that time.

Years ago I had done quite a bit of scrapbooking. During that period, I discovered a journal my maternal grandfather had written which focused quite a bit on his immigration from Sweden to America and his life thereafter. It was an immigrant journal which included a great deal of his own spiritual journey as well. I had incorporated that journal with some family photos into a scrapbook focused on him. It was my way of getting to know my grandfather whom I had never known, since he died during the 1918 flu epidemic, long before I was born. It was to that scrapbook that I turned for information when I took this, my last stab, at genealogy!

The weekend had been difficult. I needed to make a decision about my work which required wisdom beyond the available facts. Just surviving financially could very well have been at stake as a result of that decision. As I felt feelings of panic whelming up within me, I began to doubt myself spiritually! My prayers for guidance seemed to reach deaf ears, or was it my own ears which were deaf to God's voice? Then as I leafed through the pages of my scrapbook, something my grandfather had written in 1896 stood out like a divinely illuminated text:

> As my thoughts wander on the sea of life, I take my pen to write a few lines about the experiences of this year. The largest memory in my mind is that my heart is full of thanks to our Savior Who helped us through the year. If Satan tries to close the way to the earning of a decent living here in Chicago, the Master will thwart him … (translated from Swedish)

As I read those words, they stood out like a beacon of light. They seemed to be written almost for me. A man I had never known now influenced me deeply. God would indeed lead me. So far the answer was not "Yes" or "No"; it was "Wait." "Wait" is an answer too! Also, for the first time I had a personal and loving relationship with a grandfather I would not directly meet until Heaven. That felt especially good, since my maternal grandmother had died when I was one, and I never knew my father's parents.

Two days later I woke up in the middle of the night with a sense of acute anxiety over the decision I had to make. Once again I pleaded with God for guidance. Once again the silence prevailed. Then everything came together in what I choose to call an epiphany. The answer was "No." A flood of relief swept over me. My decision was made. My grandfather was right. God had triumphed over Satan and would triumph in the coming days.

Telling the story of one's journey, as is in fashion today, always seemed to me to be the province of the rich and famous or those who have lived through harrowing experiences. Now that I can see the influence on me from one simple immigrant farmer in Wisconsin, I can feel my way to understanding the importance of shared life experiences, especially in the times in which we live.

My family was Swedish-American with a strong Midwestern influence: homemade pepparkoker cookies, my mother's special apple pie, frequent home-cooked dinners served on a white table cloth with a bowl of flowers from our garden, enjoyable afternoons spent with aunts and uncles, decorating Christmas cookies with my mother, and always having a family dog and cat to play with, as well as a duck, fish, bird, rabbit, turtle and a fluctuating array of other creatures.

My mother, Elisabeth Alvera Bengtsson Skoglund,

and my father, Ragnar Emmanuel Skoglund, were both born in 1899; my mother in Necedah, Wisconsin, and my father in Stockholm, Sweden. By the time I was born in Chicago, Illinois, in 1937, the world had changed more rapidly during just that first part of the twentieth century than it had changed during the two centuries before. I was born in a hospital, my parents were born at home. Relatives who grew up with horse-drawn buggies now drove motor cars. My paternal grandfather was the first in his block on the south side of Chicago to install electric lights in his home. Even by 1911, when my father had immigrated to America, it was on a substantial "modern" ship, the Laurentic I, as compared to the small, fragile-looking ship, the Baltic I, which brought my maternal grandfather here in 1880. Progress was speeding up in that century, and the next, at a pace which has not lessened in this twenty-first century.

When the changing, unsettled yet challenging times we live in seem to be escalating too rapidly, I remember often the words of a Rabbi-friend: "God Himself presides over you in history and allows you the knowledge that He wants you to have and thinks is appropriate for you and for every generation. ... The environment that I'm in is the one that is best for my trip."

Referring to the chaos and worldwide change which was occurring on Christmas Day, 1939, as the

Nazis swept across Europe, King George VI quoted Minnie Louise Haskins:

> I said to the man who stood at the gate of the year, "Give me a light that I may tread safely into the darkness." And he replied, "Go out into the darkness and put your hand into the hand of God. That shall be to you better than light and safer than a known way."[1]

Perhaps never in the history of mankind has that quote been more applicable than in this twenty-first century in which we live.

Near the end of the 1990s, I had just moved my counseling practice into a new building. I had also just bought my first computer on the same weekend. On that Sunday afternoon as I sat with my daughter in my office, my mind spaced off all the way from the practical details of setting up an office to how amazing it was to be able to reach out to the whole world through a device sitting on a desk in a plain, ordinary room, in an average-looking office building in Burbank, California. I was almost unable to absorb all the change.

Then I remembered an incident which I had never really understood. The year was 1977. Praying with some friends in a small group, a man whom I had known to be godly uttered a prophetic word relating to me. He had been an encouragement to me in my writing and was greatly respected in his church and community. Those of us who were praying had Baptist, Presbyterian and even Plymouth Brethren backgrounds. None of us were inclined to be overtly emotional in our church services or private devotions.

The words given that afternoon to me were essentially: "You will influence people from rooms without walls." Computers were not yet mass marketed. They were not yet part of everyday conversation. Therefore none of us present on that particular afternoon had a clue about what the words meant and nobody connected them with the Internet. Keep in mind, it was just the early seventies.

As time has gone by, their meaning has became clear. Because of our access to electronic communications, our ability to influence people is powerful. "Go ye into all the world and preach the Gospel" is a command which can be obeyed from one small room. "Rooms without walls." Audible books, books on hand-held devices, televised events from around the world: these are just examples. And for those of us who deal in words, the Rabbi's statement becomes even more relevant: "God Himself presides over you in history and allows you the knowledge that He wants you to have and thinks is appropriate for you and for every generation. ... The environment that I'm in is the one that is best for my trip." That has been proven true in my life throughout the years. What better time for a writer or journalist, and anyone who enters a thought on the Internet. What a terrible, heavy responsibility for each one of us. Our words go out further than ever before in the history of mankind. Not only does God record them, but man does also.

When I was about three years old, our family moved from Chicago to California so that as the United States moved closer to full involvement in World War II, my father could work in defense at Lockheed. During that early time in California, our family attended a church in downtown Los Angeles, the Church of the Open Door. The church was huge. It had several balconies, and across the front ceiling, extending behind the pulpit and covering a large part of the front of the sanctuary, was an enormous map of the world with lights scattered here and there on different countries. Each light indicated the location of various missionaries from the church. During the Sunday services certain lights on the map would turn on, indicating which missionaries were to be especially prayed for that week.

Missionary endeavor was a major focus of that church. The exhortation to reach the whole world for Christ was often preached from the pulpit. With somewhat greater than three-year-old skepticism, I remember accepting that exhortation as an obligation from God, but feeling unsure of how the whole world could be reached. If that map was correct, it would be a big challenge.

Then at the age of 12 I attended the first major Billy Graham Crusade, the "tent crusade," located in Los Angeles. I remember the enormous tent, the sawdust floor and the crowds. Maybe this was how God would reach the world, I thought, through large meetings with Christ-filled, dynamic speakers. But that large map at church never left my consciousness, with its challenge of preaching the Gospel to all those people, especially those from many remote areas.

Then came the Internet. From individual missionaries, to large crusades, to an invention which in theory could transfer information to the whole world at one time: that was a major step forward toward preaching the Gospel to all the world. It is awesome to think that you and I, and those who come after us, have been entrusted with being born in a time of history which possesses that kind of opportunity to reach the whole world for God and to build up the Church from one little room anywhere to the most remote parts of the world. Why now? Why not a long time ago? What would David Livingstone or Charles Spurgeon have done with that kind of power? But the age-old dilemma of why is answered with the words of Abraham: "Shall not the Judge of all the earth do right?" And the responsibility to reach the world for Christ is still ours, as is the challenge of using writing and teaching as tools to encourage and build up the

Church, wherever that Church might be. We just have more to work with. That is the challenge of the twenty-first century and on, until our Lord returns.

Two

Light Through the Darkness

It was Friday. Sitting on the edge of the sloping green grass separating the UCLA main library and Royce Hall, I had to admit to myself something was wrong. The fatigue I felt was closer to pain than it was to ordinary end-of-the-week tiredness. And this wasn't the first time I had felt this way. I did have to do something about it. It wasn't going away on its own.

I had just graduated with my BA in January and was into a full load of graduate classes. I should have noticed before this that something was wrong. Just a week earlier I had been taking a test in my favorite class, Nineteenth Century American Literature, from one of my two favorite UCLA professors from my undergraduate days, Dr. Leon Howard. After reading one of the questions several times, it still didn't make sense to me, so I walked over to his desk and asked him to explain it. His answer was one of concern: "Are you okay, Betty?" Embarrassed, I faked that I was fine. When I went home that afternoon, my temperature was 102 degrees. When I got the test back the next week, I read what he had written above the "B-": "Not bad for the shape you were in." Something was definitely wrong.

But what?

Now as I sat thinking, I remembered that this was the weekend that InterVarsity Christian Fellowship was having a weekend retreat in Big Bear. Some of my friends were going and a favorite speaker of mine, Eric Fife, would be an inspiration. Quickly I gathered my things together and got a ride with a friend who was also taking the speaker up the mountain to the retreat. Even the ride itself was relaxing. Dr. Fife, who was British, began to ask me about American views on dating with questions which obviously embarrassed the driver, whom I had dated. But for me the conversation was interesting and the scenery of forest and mountain relaxing. I began to forget about how tired I had felt. This weekend away had been a wise decision.

Friday evening as the speaker gave a challenging message against the backdrop of a roaring fire in a massive stone fireplace, I began to get sleepy. At the point where I could no longer focus on the message, I decided to go back to the dormitory-type room and go to bed. "I'd feel better in the morning," I thought.

Once in bed I gradually began to wake up with feelings of tension and anxiety. As other students noisily piled in to go to bed, I faked sleep until all was quiet and the lights were out. Then, unable to endure the tension any longer, I went into an empty bathroom area and prayed. I was sure I was cracking up. "Just get me through this night, Lord," I prayed, "and I promise to go to a psychiatrist tomorrow." Finally I slept.

The next day I felt exhausted and ill but not as anxious. Not wanting a repeat of the previous night, I faked a reason to go home. Conveniently, the same person who had driven me up the mountain now had to leave in order to drive Dr. Fife down to another speaking engagement which had been a prior commitment.

That Friday afternoon at UCLA was perhaps the first time that I fully realized I had something wrong. There were to be many "last times" involved before I was diagnosed. Up to my college graduation I had enjoyed activities like basketball, tennis, hiking and skating. Those all rapidly dropped off, leaving the one remaining sport which I enjoyed, swimming. My life changed drastically from a malady which in some ways was to be the worst blow of my life – or at least the most pervasive.

Tennis went first. One evening my friend Robert and I went to a nearby tennis court and began to play. My uncle Dave had taught me to play tennis when I was 12 and then bought me my first tennis racket. I had loved tennis ever since. As Robert and I began our first game, I thought about what a lovely balmy evening it was. Perfect for an outdoor sport. Then with no warning it hit. My legs felt weak and then began to give out. As I started to collapse, Robert grabbed me just in time to avoid a complete fall. Once in the car,

I can still remember the relief of leaning back from sheer exhaustion. Then I realized how weak my legs felt. There was almost no muscle tone, no strength. By the time we reached home, I could feel a little bit of strength coming back into my legs but not enough to walk. Robert half carried me into my house where lying in bed eventually restored me. And so it went: things I could never do again, slow recovery from activities I used to do without thinking, and a relentless fatigue which no amount of rest seemed to relieve.

Years later this attack on my body was finally given a name: Chronic Fatigue Syndrome. Getting to that diagnosis was not easy however. At first I always thought it would go away with more rest, but it didn't. Doctors didn't know a lot about Chronic Fatigue Syndrome at that time; and unknown disorders like what I had often fell into the more vague psychological category. But as one psychologist admitted, "It's not psychological, but it's real and just might be something not yet known by medical science." Several physicians thought of thyroid, Addison's disease, rheumatic fever, myasthenia gravis – to name a few. Treating hypoglycemia and trying alternative medicine didn't make any positive difference. Then a new physician said to me: "We could run thousands of dollars in tests and find nothing, because I believe you have Chronic Fatigue Syndrome, for which there is no test or cure." In some odd way that statement brought peace. It didn't cure me, but as he explained the symptoms to me I knew he was right. At least it had a name. Maybe someday it would have a cure.

Chronic Fatigue Syndrome is among the worst things that have ever happened to me. It makes any other illness harder; it stops most athletic activities except moderate or short walks; it limits the length of a workday; and one feels continually lazy. At its worst I compare the fatigue with pain. Yet one Bible verse always resonates in my mind: "Shall not the Judge of all the earth do right?" The answer is a resounding "yes." And at least now most doctors who have done their research acknowledge the reality of the disease. Research is escalating and even Social Security Disability has acknowledged its existence and the Red Cross does not want blood donations from people with Chronic Fatigue Syndrome.

Off the coast of Pacific Grove, California, between Monterey and Carmel By The Sea, stands an old lighthouse, Point Pinos. Right beyond the lighthouse is the sea. When I was a child, up through my teens, my parents and I used to spend our summer vacations at a motel around the corner from the lighthouse. It was called Butterfly Trees Lodge because every year Monarch Butterflies would migrate to those trees and continue their cycle of life.

I would often wander down the dirt road in front of the lighthouse to a huge rock that jutted out into the sea. Establishing myself comfortably on the far end of the rock, I watched the ocean splashing up against it while I thought and prayed. It was my secret place with God. I prayed a lot about God's future plans for my life, wanting His will but also begging Him to let me go to the mission field and start a school or an orphanage, particularly with the Chinese.

Chronic Fatigue Syndrome stopped that goal, I could say. But did it really stop GOD'S goal? Without Chronic Fatigue Syndrome I might never have written books that understand people's suffering. I would probably not have ever done counseling because most of my church friends spiritualized emotional pain and in many ways I shared their viewpoint until I got Chronic Fatigue Syndrome. It was from a "shrink" that I first realized that I wasn't imagining my debilitating fatigue – it wasn't in my head; it was a physical disorder which was probably as yet unknown.

Chronic Fatigue Syndrome was not some giant mistake God made in an off moment. It was something He used to make me into someone who would understand and help people. He didn't want me to start a school or orphanage. But He did want me to teach and then to write and do psychotherapy. And, by the way, what better time to write than in the electronic age.

Someday maybe they'll find a cure for this debilitating disease. I would love that. But while so far it has been the most difficult situation I have ever had to deal with, I know God has used it for the major course of my life to gently nudge me in the direction of His choice.

THREE

Where Are They Now?

I couldn't have picked a more interesting time to be a high school teacher and counselor than the sixties. During my first two years, I taught English at Marlborough, an exclusive, private girls school in Los Angeles. I was 21, teaching senior English to girls barely younger than myself. Marlborough was a perfect "first school" to teach in.

But there were unique challenges. Marlborough was a school for the rich and famous. This included everyone from children and grandchildren of world leaders and famous media people to ordinary people who had made it big in this world's eyes even though they weren't famous.

There were invitations to tea at beautiful, lavishly furnished homes, and thoughtful gifts of flowers and hand-knitted sweaters. The girls were considerate, polite, and well disciplined. As one girl put it, "After opening doors for teachers during the week, I sometimes start to open doors for a date on the weekend."

As a young teacher I loved the experience. It was new to me and challenging. I liked the students, they liked me. But then the greatest enemy in my years of teaching broke through: Boredom! These girls studied, were bright and behaved politely. But I needed more challenge. For one thing, I needed the challenge of boys and students from deprived backgrounds. I needed discipline problems and kids who hated school. I wanted to challenge teenagers who were not challenged at home, those who hadn't grown up with books or parents who read to them. I wanted to make a difference. And so for ten years I became a teacher and then a counselor at Glendale High School in Glendale, California.

Added to my fifties education and my two years in the early sixties spent in a relatively sheltered teaching experience, I was now in a sixties atmosphere of denial. While drugs flourished all over Southern California, and across the country as well, towns like Glendale didn't have a drug problem or a race issue – or so they thought. After several years of teaching English and serving as a school counselor, I was asked to start a nine-week group counseling program for tenth graders. The focus was to be on college planning. Boring, but at least different.

But as usual life didn't go as planned. The sessions quickly turned into drug counseling. There was one problem. I myself had been brought up in a sheltered time. I knew nothing about street drugs, and so for about six months I read a lot and above all listened until I knew the terminology. LSD, acid, was big at that time, as was marijuana or weed, grass, pot. PCP was called "angel dust" in those days. And the various forms of cocaine were too expensive for most.

For the last year of my sojourn with high school students in a school setting, I established a state-mandated program for students who were classified as "emotionally handicapped." Translated, that meant the kids that didn't fit anywhere else. There was a girl who wandered around the classroom talking to someone only she saw; a savant, who was extraordinarily gifted in music; a borderline mentally retarded young man; a drug user and dealer for whom I made a pot of coffee each morning so he could stay awake; and 15 others with distinct but different problems which made them stand out from the general school population. It was up to me to develop some kind of individualized curriculum for which I was given several thousand useless dollars for supplies. Useless, because all orders had to be put through certain required channels, which in themselves took months. Ultimately, I spent my own money and also found discarded books which smelled like smoke from a fire the previous summer. It was challenging and yet rewarding. I really cared about those kids. But when I left teaching forever that May, in defense of my seemingly quick decision the Superintendent of the District commented: "What else could she do; she's done it all."

Yet in the decades I have spent as a psychotherapist

and author I have never forgotten those students, and, in turn, sporadically some of us have kept in touch. Early on, I realized I could never really walk away when I picked up my phone late one evening and heard a familiar voice on the other end: "You F...ing B." "I wish I had never met you. You're a phony, and I hate you. F U. By now you should hate me. Hate me," she screamed.

"Why?" I replied quietly.

"Don't you get it," she said. "I want to die. I want to kill myself, but I can't do that as long as you care. No one else cares. My parents sure don't. They would be happy to get rid of me. Just hate me! Please," she ended with a sob.

Sue had taken large amounts of every drug except heroin and showed her self-hate openly. She burned herself with cigarette butts. She was always saying something like, "I'm stupid and ugly and even my family can't stand me." Then, when anyone complimented her or pointed out some of her strengths, she became angry and cut them off. During the period of time I knew her, she insulted me, shocked me with stories of her behavior and wanted me to see her stoned on every drug imaginable – to "prove" to me that she was worthless. She tried to make me agree with her low opinion of herself. She told me repeatedly that I was the only human being who had not agreed with her and sooner or later she would convince me of her worthlessness and hopelessness.

I remembered another day, back when I was still teaching, and she had called me for help. She was home alone, wishing someone was there with her. Her parents were at a party and thought she was just acting like a teenager. I drove to her house to make sure she was okay and let her know she was not some neglected brat, which is what she felt like. I never met her parents although I wanted to scream at them to act like parents, hold her, comfort her. Sometimes when I got one of my middle of the night calls and felt almost too tired to work the next day, I wanted to really scream at many parents. Their kids were wonderful but mixed up and hurting. Sue didn't kill herself and we kept in touch for a while. I still hope that somewhere, sometime, she found the One who searches out the lost and invites them to come to Him.

The problem was some of these parents were no better off, maybe worse. One girl who needed love and support went home from school one day to find her mother drunk and dead on the floor. At the end of the year on my birthday, she and her friend gave me a gold charm engraved to me. Yet I had done so little. There was so little I could do.

Maybe the fact that I could help so limitedly is a basic reason that I ultimately left working in the schools. Sometimes I felt like I was applying Band-Aids when major surgery was needed. Groups amounting to several hundred students a year, time restrictions on one-to-one encounters, heart-wrenching stories, midnight crisis phone calls all took their toll. Images remain in my mind and haunt me when I think of them. I remember standing on the balcony outside of my classroom one afternoon, watching a girl who had talked with me often slowly enter the school yard, sober, beaten down, tear stained. I can still see the entrance, the pathway, the course she took as she came toward the building I was in. My heart ached for her as I realized she was coming back within a couple of hours from having an abortion she hadn't wanted.

Working in a school setting also involved legal complications. I became known as a person who knew a lot about what was going on in the school, particularly in the area of drugs. One day a school administrator approached me and told me that he wanted me to come to him after school each day and tell him what various students were doing, particularly in the area of drugs. Stunned and a little intimidated, I replied, "How long do you think I'll be in business at that rate?" Ignoring the question, he insisted again on my being a narc for the school. I refused. I went to the Board of Education and talked to one of the Superintendents. His response was that I was taking the correct approach and that to follow the administrator's instructions could cause me to be sued by a parent. Reassured, I continued as I had before.

At this time the unions were just starting to become

involved in the district but many of us teachers had shown no interest in joining. Somehow, however, they got involved in my situation without my ever even meeting them, much less joining or even asking for help. They made it clear to the administration that I was to be left alone in terms of reporting and that in no way was I to be discriminated against because of this action. Frankly, I was very nervous about subtle slights and comments, but instead the air seemed to have cleared and I was treated very well. I was relieved because as long as I stayed at Glendale High School I hoped to be able to help some of these lost kids who were trying to find their way.

There were so many. Richard, who lived on drugs but was so bright, so full of potential, graduated to prison rather than walking down the aisle at graduation. There were a couple of calls for help from both Richard and his mother. A letter or two went to a judge, who decided that if I would guarantee therapy for Richard, he could be let out and given another chance. A number of years after the therapy, another call came through to me. This time Richard was in jail again, for perhaps the stupidest reason ever. Standing in a parking lot with a friend, the friend turned to him and said: "Hey Rich, could you take that box out of my car and put it in the back of Joey's truck over there."

"Sure," responded Richard agreeably. In minutes he was in handcuffs. Arrested for transporting illegal drugs. His "friend" was nowhere to be seen. Jail once again.

The calls for help started once more: first from his mother and then from Richard himself. But when I spoke to Richard on the phone, this time I sensed a hesitancy, something I couldn't define. After talking a little while I bluntly asked Richard if he really wanted to get out of jail. Did he want to change?

"Is this what YOU really want," I asked, "or is it just your mother this time?" At that point, Richard explained his real feelings, Jail had become home. He would miss it if he were outside. Sadly, I knew he was telling the truth about his real feelings.

I've never heard from Richard since that call. I have no idea where he is or if he's even alive. That haunts me still. The so-called hippies of the sixties were lost kids, many of them from rich families who were too busy making money to care or even know what was happening to their kids. At least that's how many of their teenage kids felt. I loved those lost kids. At least they knew their lives were empty and that their parents' lives were empty. They were searching for meaning and ended up finding it in blotting out reality through drugs, much as their parents had done the same through alcohol. One teenager expressed her feeling well in a poem:

What if I had a problem?

> Could I talk to you?
> Even if it was something you
>   couldn't understand?
> Could I tell you my problems of
>   sex or parents or God?
> Would you listen?

And, then, to answer her own question after finding someone she could talk to:

> I sat in the middle of my mind today,
> I had to figure out my head.
> I wanted you to know because you'll
>   listen to me.
> You'll listen – and you won't condemn.
>
> My head is swimming around in confusion.
> Who is God … Why do we cry … What
>   is love … How can we know?
> You can always help me by being
>   around … and you are.
> You're easy to be with,
> I can talk at my own speed.

Her words express, better than I can, what some of today's teenagers look for: someone who will really listen to them talk at their own speed. Maybe that's what all of us look for from time to time.

FOUR

Guides and Mentors

Hymn writer Francis R. Havergal was very fond of mountain climbing and engaged in it frequently. At times when the terrain was difficult or unknown, she and a few friends would attempt a particularly challenging climb and in the process use a guide who was experienced. He knew what lay ahead. He hiked in front of them. They developed skill and also avoided danger by following his every step. The guide protected them from danger, but he was not particularly attached to any one person in the group. It was his job. Indeed, sometimes they were people he had never known before.

In the area of spiritual nurturing, in the day in which we live we are perhaps likely to confuse the difference in meaning between the words *mentor* and *guide*.

Those who influenced me when I was a young child were mainly members of my own family, teachers at church and eventually at school. When I was around four years old, my aunt Ruth came home on furlough from China where she had served for a number of years as a missionary under the CIM, the

China Inland Mission. My aunt and I became very close and she became an early mentor in my life. As a young child, I shared part of her passion for spreading the Gospel of Jesus Christ. I also developed a special love for the Chinese people and well into my teens I had a deep desire to be a missionary in China and start an orphanage or school in that country. Then health issues made me wonder if that would even be possible.

As I grew into my teens, my parents thought that a smaller school might be easier for me physically, and so in ninth grade I was enrolled in Culter Academy, a small Christian school in Los Angeles. A teacher at the school offered me a ride, and when he was not available, I adjusted quite quickly to the three buses and one streetcar required to get to school and back. I didn't mind the trip and soon learned to use my commute time to study. That way I could have more free time at home. I liked the routine better than the long walk to the local public school.

On my first day at Culter, I went through the usual procedures of signing up for classes and meeting people. The first step, as I recall, was meeting my new school principal, Miss Pamela Reeve. She looked pleasant but strict and I basically liked her. Little did I know that she was to become a lifelong mentor. As is so often true of mentors, Miss Reeve started out as a guide, someone who was helpful. She was a wonderful teacher in history, but I did not at this time view her as a mentor, as someone I would have trusted with normal teenage issues. After all, she was still a teacher and, on top of that, a principal. As it turned out, she was to become one of the main mentors of my life, a process which was gradual.

After I left Culter and finished my senior year at Burbank High School in order to graduate with my early childhood friends, I realized the strong mentor connection I had with Miss Reeve, by then Pam to me. I look back on one rather silly conversation I had with her that only a mentor who cared – not merely a guide who was doing their duty – would have bothered with. Pam and I were at a weekend retreat. There were no scheduled meetings for the afternoon, so Pam and I took a walk in a nearby field. "Pam," I said. "Do you think that if I love someone, God will cause him to love me too because of my leading in that direction? Would He lead us in different paths or the same?" She didn't laugh at my naivety but took me seriously and gently pointed out reality to me. Nor did that mentor role change when she moved to Oregon to become Dean of Women at Multnomah Bible College.

Another mentor I had from my Culter days was Beverly West, my high school Bible and English teacher. While Pam was my closer confidant, Bev introduced me to most of the writers I still most cherish: Amy Carmichael, Hudson Taylor, H. C. G. Moule, and others. My dates became trips to old bookstores! Bev ended up in Taiwan as a missionary with her surgeon husband, John. Both my relationships with Pam and with Bev continued. They were for life.

Often the mentor relationship becomes practical as well as extending. Because of my frequent strep throats and high fevers, finally, at the age of 22, I had my tonsils removed. After I had spent a week at home recovering, Pam invited me to spend the weekend at her home to break the monotony, also inviting a friend of mine from my high school years. At that time in her life Pam was counseling at Glendale College and I was teaching at Marlborough, a private girls school in Los Angeles.

For me it was a relief to be in a new atmosphere. It was a lovely, balmy summer evening. We sat outside on the patio and ate, talked and, in today's vernacular, "hung out." I seemed fine, certainly less bored than I had been all week. Pam's gesture of hospitality had been welcome and generous, but not surprising. I had known her since I was 14 when I was at Culter Academy, and the friend/mentoring relationship was of lifetime duration. She always gave more than she took.

That night I woke up suddenly with bleeding in my throat from my recent surgery. The result was re-hospitalization. I can remember the scene as well now as when it happened: a doctor looking at my throat and telling me I had a blood clot which would have to be surgically removed. Then the clot broke loose on its own. Sitting on a chair in the room, Pam absolutely refused to leave and go home. All I could think of was that it was the middle of the night and she had to go to work the next day. "I'll go when you're asleep," she kept saying. I knew that would take a while. I also knew that she would not change her mind. Eventually, in desperation I decided to fake it. I made myself look very asleep. Soon I heard her get up from her chair and come over to the bed. Quietly she peered down at me and walked around the bed. I lay there afraid to breathe. Satisfied that I was asleep, she silently left the room. Soon I slept. She had not been easy to fool.

It is not simple to choose which memories of either Bev or Pam to write about. There are so many. At Culter they were each the kind but somewhat strict principal/teacher types. Yet the relationship was always that of a confidant, a friendly advisor.

With each the relationship continued throughout college, into my teaching years and throughout the rest of my life. Each included going to weekend retreats, attending Bible studies rich with Bible teaching and the singing of all of those wonderful hymns from the old IVP hymn book. Added to all these were occasional short trips, often with several other friends of all ages, where we had fun, usually in the outdoor world of nature or visiting small touristy shops. But there was always the Lord, with short devotionals and long-remembered quiet one-to-one talks which were often part of a long walk in some scenic spot.

I have had my own private counseling practice for years now and have written a number of books which usually include some discussion of wholeness. Unlike many in the Christian world who spiritualize emotional problems, both Bev and Pam understood that we truly are body, mind and spirit, and so I have felt their lifelong support of what I have been doing now for some 50 years. I don't know that I ever felt that support more than when each of them called me a short while before they died to say "Goodbye" in terms of this earth. On this earth they were truly mentors. Their going HOME is Heaven's gain and earth's loss.

Mentors come in different shapes and sizes and often our Lord uses them in very different ways. But they encourage, advise, and are usually people we admire. The most unusual mentor I ever had was Ruth Bell Graham. We never met and for a long time, as we communicated by mail and phone, we really didn't think of the relationship as a friendship. For me it all started when I was asked to do an article for a Christian magazine which involved at least one interview by phone. Ruth was agreeable, and so it started. After that we communicated when either of us felt like it until one Christmas she sent a short note on the card saying that she had realized we really were friends. We were long past the original magazine article interview.

On my side of the relationship I valued her deep godliness and wisdom. One time I told her about an incident which occurred with my aunt Ruth, a missionary in China under the China Inland Mission. She had come home from China for a furlough because of illness. One day in my teenage years, my aunt was over at my parents' home and appeared to be quite depressed. In my youthful ignorance, I told her to confess her depression. "I can't believe I said that," I remarked to Ruth. Now as a psychotherapist it really bothered me. "Oh my dear," she responded. "You were saying what you really thought at that time." She was right. Many Christians felt that way about depression in those days, and some still do. I'm not happy about saying that to my aunt, but I can let it go as youthful ignorance and not feel guilty. Ruth was special and I was blessed to know her.

Nor should we ignore the value of infrequent, even one-time, encounters. Some recent studies suggest that among the contributors to longevity are brief encounters with people whom we greet or know to a small degree, like postmen, bank clerks, post office employees, milkmen and others, famous or unknown.

Sometimes a brief encounter can influence our lives profoundly. I will never forget standing in a parking lot with John Stott, each of us waiting for a driver to pick us up. Stott was at one time Queen Elizabeth's chaplain, but is mainly remembered for his books and lectures on Christianity. I had heard him speak several times but had never just chatted with him or even met him. But in that brief wait in a parking lot his gentleness and kindness spoke volumes about the truth he uttered from the pulpit. Years later when John Stott died, I received in the mail a small carved wooden bird in a carved wooden box commemorating his life. He was a bird watcher. It stands on a shelf in a bookcase in my bedroom, a reminder of the genuineness of this godly man who noticed everyone he encountered and made them feel special, even when he never really knew them.

When I was in my early teens, I went to hear a series on the book of Romans taught by J. Sidlow Baxter, a noted speaker, author and Bible teacher. After one lecture, I asked him a question about Romans 6. He gave me the telephone number of his hotel room while his wife stood patiently by. We spent time on the phone on several different occasions that week, debating theology. I was a junior in high school, but he took time and gave it freely to answer my questions. It left an unforgettable mark on my life. Perhaps the time and interest he took for an unknown teenager made the greatest impact on me and validated his message.

Teachers, doctors, neighbors and many other people affect our lives if we let them in a little. For the Christian it not only impacts a physical lifespan but often our spiritual health.

Sometimes such encounters end in ways we could never imagine. Long after those teenage years, I discovered that Baxter had moved to the United States and was living in California. I called him one day and we had a very different but once again unforgettable conversation. As we parted, he said with a voice full of joy, "Oh Elizabeth, I cannot wait to see my Lord." Soon after he crossed the porch of Heaven to his Father's home.

> Just when Thou wilt, Thy time is best,
> Thou shalt appoint my hour of rest,
> Marked by the Sun of perfect love,
> Shining unchangeably above.
>
> Just when Thou wilt, no choice for me,
> Life is a gift to use for Thee;
> Death is a hushed and glorious tryst,
> With Thee, my King, my Savior, Christ!
> – Frances R. Havergal

The torch is now passed to us.

FIVE

The God of All Comfort

It was warm outside as I stood in front of my cabin just a few yards away from the gently rolling waves of the ocean. I had come to this tropical paradise a few days earlier with two friends. On this particular day I had spent the afternoon in town shopping while my friend Ed went to visit someone in a nearby town. My other friend Sophie preferred to stay close to the beach while she tried to absorb the trauma she was going through over her recent divorce. We were about to find out that none of us had quite comprehended how much Sophie had not recovered from the unfaithfulness of this man whom she had so deeply loved.

Like a giant orange ball, the sun was slowly descending into the bright blue water in front of me. For a moment the beauty of this place overwhelmed me. Zihuatanejo, Mexico, was a paradise of beauty. That beauty included surrounding areas: the coconut grove, the highway which extended for miles along the sea, the white sandy beach as yet unpolluted by man.

At the end of our weeks' sojourn, the magnificence of this beauty was to be shown even more as we traveled 150 miles to Acapulco. The road from Zihuatanejo to

Acapulco followed the coastline the entire way. We felt we were in another world, or at least in another time zone. We saw women who were washing their clothes in the ocean, scrubbing them on rocks by the shore, a colorful scene of laughter and camaraderie. Children played happily in the sand nearby and the stress of modern life seemed to belong to another world indeed.

Now, however, my enjoyment of the beauty of this place was just starting. In several different ways, I was about to learn a great deal about love. I turned back to the door of my room in order to grab my camera and take a quick picture of sea before the sun disappeared into the oncoming night.

As I opened the door and glanced inside the room, the tranquility of the scene behind me vanished, replaced by perplexity about what I should do. In front of me on the floor lay shattered glass from at least one broken wine glass and an empty wine bottle which was partially sticking out from under a chair. Crumpled in a groggy heap on one of the beds was Sophie, attempting to give an appearance of sobriety as she saw me enter the room. The rage was there, too, as she threw another empty glass on the floor, angry now because she had no more wine and had nowhere to go for more. Resigned to the inevitable, she groggily announced that she was going to sleep and promptly did so.

Later that evening things were still not going well. We were in a primitive part of the world where there was little or no access to medical care or any other kind of help. In view of the situation at hand, that fact made me nervous. What if Sophie needed help? But I suspected Sophie just needed sleep – and no more alcohol.

For now, however, more relevant to my needs, Sophie was drunk and difficult to deal with, even potentially violent. She was unpredictable, and yet when we left her alone she did sleep. Her agitation increased when either Ed or I tried to help. Since even our efforts to clean up the mess seemed to upset her, we gave up on that for the moment and eventually went outside.

"I can't protect you here," Ed said to me as we sat outside by the ocean, sipping hot coffee and talking. "My room is too far away. The only way for me to protect you is for you to stay with me tonight. And this is not some kind of excuse to try to seduce you," he added.

I trusted Ed. We knew each other well, and there was a great deal of affection and respect which existed between us. He admired my commitment to Christ, and I longed for him to share in that belief. But Ed had been brought up in a strict Christian home, too strict, and the scars of resentment remained. Even though I loved Ed more than I had loved any other man, I could never have married him because of that spiritual barrier. I had loved before, but until I met Ed I don't believe I had ever been truly "in love."

Nothing physical happened that night: just two beds and two exhausted people sleeping. But I experienced a feeling of safety and being cared for that one rarely experiences in this world. As one of Ed's friends said to me later, the emotions of caring which existed in the room that night were more than many people experience in an entire marriage. God had given me comfort in the middle of a difficult situation. Without any physical contact between Ed and me, God gave me an even greater gift, a sense of the potential of a God-ordained relationship between a man and a woman who love each other.

There was something else I learned in Mexico: what Mexicans are really like. Many of us have a stereotypical view of the sombrero over the face, leaning against a wall, sleeping while others work. Or drugs slipped across the border and illegal aliens who rip us off. In Zihuatanejo I found people who were friendly, hardworking and caring.

I noticed that even though many families lived in poverty, when the weather was at the peak of its humidity and heat, families often ate outside under the shelter of palm trees. Laughter rang out as the children interacted with their families. Many of the men had worked throughout the heat of the afternoon but still enjoyed their families.

Kindness was also extended to strangers. After Ed

and I had finally been able to clean up the mess from Sophie's drinking binge and I had been able to go back to my room the next day, the maid who had always been extremely nice to both Ed and myself gave me a lovely bouquet of flowers. I think she understood more than we knew what had happened and respected how we had handled it.

On another occasion I got eaten up by mosquitoes, to which I was allergic. At dinner that night my bites slowly became large welts, itchy and red. Late that evening, when I was back in my cabin, a young man who had served at dinner knocked at my door. "Here," he said as he handed me an armful of burned leaves, "rub these over your bites and you'll sleep better." He was right. But above all once again a stranger had cared.

God delights in providing comfort and love for His earthly children. As part of that provision, for most people God ordains marriage. Early on in the Bible we are told that it is not good for man (or woman?) to live alone. Almost anyone can find someone to marry. To find the RIGHT person is more difficult; and in my opinion singleness is preferable to marriage to the wrong person. For a few, singleness is an actual calling from God, usually relating to a life work. A good biblical example is the Apostle Paul. Although he was obviously married at one time, since he was a member of the Sanhedrin, once his wife was gone he did not remarry. Yet, in contrast, we have Priscilla and Aquila, who were married and jointly taught church leaders like Apollos.

Whatever our unique situation may be relating to marriage, God gives His comfort along the way, whether it be to the widow, the person whose marriage turns sour, the betrayed spouse or the person called to singleness. In the book of Ephesians there is the striking image of Christ as the Head of the Church, the Body of Christ. He is our Bridegroom. As such He is the Believer's greatest source of comfort and power. Furthermore, comfort along the way is something God actually delights in giving in the middle of a variety of difficult life experiences which we encounter on our journey. He rescues us, often in ways we never dreamed of.

Six

A Cup of Coffee with God

It was Sunday morning. I was preparing to go to church, but I paused as I heard a familiar sound outside. It was raining. Looking out the widow, I realized that it had been raining for quite a period of time. Water lay in little pools outside the door and a thin sheet of wetness shimmered on the pavement. The multitude of stairs beyond, combined with the rain, made an exit from the building challenging. Because of my deteriorating arthritic joints, leaving for church seemed risky.

Looking once again at the bleakness outside, I decided to change my clothes and relax. Having exchanged my dress for a dressing gown, and pouring myself a second cup of hot coffee, I settled into a comfortable recliner chair. Life was good after all, I thought. Unlike the enemy I had perceived it to be, the rain sounded friendly now, even reassuring with its steady beat on the roof above.

Then as I thought once again of missing church, it occurred to me that I had also not had my quiet time, my morning ritual of prayer and Bible reading. "Ritual?" I thought. What an odd word to use. Yet so often that was what a quiet time had felt like a few years before. Perhaps that was why I had so often forgotten to have my time alone with God or postponed its timing until later in the day. Still, during periods of crisis, prayer and portions of the Bible were always my refuge. Many of my friends had expressed similar feelings of forcing rather than wanting to pray and read their Bibles routinely before they started their day. They, too, were Christians. We loved to worship God in the taking of Holy Communion. We wanted our lives to be lived in His service. But individual Bible reading and prayer had become too routine, almost boring. Yet ironically we all went faithfully to Bible studies or meetings where the teaching was deep and analytical.

Well, I decided if I wasn't going to church, I should at least start my quiet time. I looked at the clock and determined to spend at least twenty minutes in just prayer. I hadn't really timed my prayers since I had gradually changed my approach to something I now truly enjoy. It is pretty incredible when you think about being able to talk to the God of all the universe about anything. It is even more incredible that He cares, that He is our God and yet our Heavenly Father, our best Friend, our Saviour and much more. Twenty minutes sounded good. I settled into my chair and drank a couple of sips from my cup of hot coffee. I could feel my body relax and I was grateful for the silence around me. Without my being totally aware of the positive change, there had been one. I now looked forward to having a quiet time.

A few years back when I wrote a book on people who had been especially meaningful to me spiritually, I did a chapter on the Victorian preacher/bible teacher F. B. Meyer. An illustration he used now resonated in my mind as I thought about the boldness involved in this conversational approach with God. This approach was what I meant when I began to refer to my quiet time as a cup of coffee with God. At first I had worried that it was irreverent. But Meyer seemed at least as bold.

One afternoon in a tram-car in North London, he noticed on the opposite seat an elderly woman with a basket, evidently a charwoman returning from her day's work. She appeared to be anything but happy, and as the car emptied only he and she were left. Then, having recognized him all along, she summoned up courage to speak to him and calling him by name, she told him her story. As a widow she had been left alone in the world except for her crippled daughter who, in spite of her affliction, was a continual joy to her. Every morning, as she explained, when she came home from her work she knew her daughter was in the room where they lived, ready to greet her. She was always there, and at night in the darkness she could stretch out her hand and know she was there, too. She made tea in the morning, and left her for the day, but she knew all the time that her daughter was there to greet her with a glad face when she returned. "And now," she said sadly, "now she is dead, and I am alone, and I am miserable. I am going home, and it is scarcely home, for she is not there."

There was little time for discussion, but Meyer was "At Attention!" for his Master on the moment. "When you get home and put the key in the door," he said, "say aloud, 'Jesus, I know You are here,' and be ready to greet Him directly when you open the door. And as you light the fire tell Him what has happened during the day; if anybody has been kind, tell Him, if anybody has been unkind, tell Him, just as you would have told your daughter. Be sure to make your cup of tea. At night stretch out your hand in the darkness and say, 'Jesus, I know You are here.'" Then the tram-car reached the terminus, and they parted.[1]

A few months later Meyer was on the same tram-car again. A woman greeted him.

"You won't know me, Mr. Meyer," she said.

"I am afraid I do not," he replied. Then she reminded him of the interview some months before. "But you are not the same woman," he said in astonishment. "Oh, yes, I am," she said. "I did as you told me. I went home and said, 'Jesus, I know You are here,' and I kept saying it, and it has made all the difference in my life, and now I feel I know Him."[2]

It is remarkable to be able to have those early moments in any day spent with the God of the universe, our Heavenly Father Who loves us, our Shepherd Who leads us. There could be no greater privilege than to start our day with a cup of coffee, or tea or hot chocolate, with God.

Way back in my life I had heard many say that they usually read their Bibles first and then prayed, but I had found it to be more effective for me to pray first and then read. For prayer is work, while I feel fed from the Scriptures. I'm sure there are, however, good arguments on both sides.

By now, as I had begun to try to make my personal time with God more meaningful, I began to establish a routine around prayer which started out with confession, praise, and worship. Somewhere toward the beginning of this prayer time came confession of any sin, known and unknown. There was praise for the day, for God's graciousness and blessing. Then from a grateful, cleansed heart could come worship of God for Who He is in His perfection, holiness and power.

As an aside, I have learned that God handles bluntness quite well as long as that bluntness remains reverent. When I was in my first year of teaching in a local high school, I received a very low rating for my first few months of teaching. I thought I had done a good job, certainly not a failing job. Then the situation was explained to me by the principal of the school who had just found out himself. The woman in the school who had given the rating was jealous of the woman at the Board of Education who had recommended me to the school in the first place. My friend at the Board had gotten the job the other woman wanted. Being in the middle of their feud had caused me to get the low rating. It was her revenge. When those higher up found out about the situation, I was completely exonerated.

Driving home from work on the day that I had just found out the whole story, I could feel my anger rising. Perhaps once declared innocent I felt safe enough to feel that anger. "Forgive me Lord for this rage," I prayed. But it still sat there. Once again I tried. Nothing. Finally I was honest, blunt if you want to call it that. "Dear Lord," I prayed. "I don't want to give up my anger. I don't want you to take it." Now that I had been so justified by everyone, I enjoyed hating this horrible woman even more. But there was no peace. At last I prayed, "Dear Lord, I can't change my feelings, but I can change my action. So I give you this hate and I take your love." I didn't feel anything change in my feelings, but I felt able to leave feelings and go on, just trusting God for the right ones.

The next day at school, at snack time in the cafeteria, I got my cup of coffee and turned to join my friends. They were all at one table. My abuser was at another table alone, as she usually was, in spite of her power. "No, God," I said quietly to myself as I realized how God was leading me. "That's too much," I continued. Then I realized if I were to follow God I had no choice. I joined her for coffee. Coffee with my enemy. After that act of obedience, the rage left and pity took its place. I never trusted her, but I cared. When I left the school eight years later to be a psychotherapist, we parted as friends and exchanged greetings from time to time over the years.

In my new way of having a quiet time, and more specifically, my new way of praying, intercessory prayer was the next thing I worked on, starting out by making changes to my "hit or miss" approach. It has developed into something much more organized, while it remains flexible under the leading of the Holy Spirit. I usually start praying for my family and then for the local church I attend, for the established leadership and any who lead but are not formally identified with a title. I then pray for those I feel led to remember in or outside of this local body of Believers. Sometimes my prayer arises from my own sense of leading and at other times I go by someone's request for prayer.

I have only recently, however, started using a written list. This list helps keep me accountable in faithfulness to pray where I have made that promise. It also helps me remember any specifics and reminds me of current changes to include in my prayer. For example, a request for successful cancer treatment turns into praise when that success has occurred. Taking prayer this seriously is also a deterrent for any tendency to lightly skip a day or ignore the task of follow through. It becomes part of a serious work within the Church, the Body of Christ. In the course of church history, it has always been a serious work. It is not always viewed that way today, however, in the activist society in which we live.

Years ago, when I was just in my teens, there was a dear older women in the church I attended who was often a guide or mentor to those of us who were considered the young people in the church. One morning she said to several of us that she had found a verse which said we were to pray "combatingly." She then went on to quote Colossians 4:12, using the J. N. Darby version. As I studied that verse, I went beyond Darby to other translators whom I also respected. I saw that according to Weymouth, one of my favorite translators, Darby's word "combatingly" is translated "wrestling," and in Rotherham's translation it reads "contending in your behalf in his prayers." In the King

James Version it reads "labouring fervently." The use of these more aggressive words implies a very active work. When we ask for prayer, the biblical context for that request implies hard work. When we commit to pray for someone, that promise shouldn't be communicated in a bored word or two or through a simple emoji on a cell phone without any words added. To pray means labor, time, passion. We can't always dedicate large pieces of time or energy to a single prayer request. But the commitment to pray should never be casual. One moment of prayer should at least go beyond a mere emoji on a computer or a guilty "please bless." On the other hand, a brief "please save him" uttered with passion as someone is falling off a roof means more than a long grocery list prayed without passion. In our quiet time, even when a request has to be short but is yet prayed for combatingly, as though in battle, it is effective. Balance of time and intensity, under the direction of God, is also part of the Christian life. Usually burnout is not meant to be.

Apart from our own level of passion, God has His own expectation. He wants us to care enough about the subject matter of our prayers to pray persistently, to plead, to pursue. Many years ago D.L. Moody wrote the following encouraging words:

In Luke's Gospel we have as a grand supplement to the "Disciples' Prayer," "Ask, and it shall be given you; seek, and ye shall find; knock, and it shall be opened unto you." Some people think God does not like to be troubled with our constant coming and asking. The only way to trouble God is not to come at all. He encourages us to come to Him repeatedly, and press our claims. ...

"Teacher," said a bright, earnest-faced boy, "why is it that so many prayers are unanswered? I do not understand. The Bible says, 'Ask, and ye shall receive; seek, and ye shall find; knock, and it shall be opened unto you;' but it seems to me a great many knock and are not admitted."

"Did you never sit by your cheerful parlor fire," said the teacher, "on some dark evening, and hear a loud knocking at the door? Going to answer the summons, have you not sometimes looked out into the darkness, seeing nothing, but hearing the pattering feet of some mischievous boy, who knocked but did not wish to enter, and therefore ran away? Thus is it often with us. We ask for blessings, but do not really expect them; we knock, but do not mean to enter; we fear that Jesus will not hear us, will not fulfil His promises, will not admit us; and so we go away."

"Ah, I see," said the earnest-faced boy, his eyes shining with the new light dawning in his soul: "Jesus cannot be expected to answer runaway knocks. He has never promised it. I mean to keep knocking, knocking, until He *cannot help opening the door."*

Too often we knock at mercy's door, and then run away, instead of waiting for an entrance and an answer.[3]

A woman, whose encounter with Christ is described in both Matthew and Mark, is a wonderful example of persistence in prayer.

And, behold, a woman of Canaan came out of the same coasts, and cried unto him, saying, Have mercy on me, O Lord, thou Son of David; my daughter is grievously vexed with a devil. But he answered her not a word. And his disciples came and besought him, saying, Send her away; for she crieth after us. But he answered and said, I am not sent but unto the lost sheep of the house of Israel. Then came she and worshipped him, saying, Lord, help me. But he answered and said, It is not meet to take the children's bread, and to cast it to dogs. And she said, Truth, Lord: yet the dogs eat of the crumbs which fall from their masters' table. Then Jesus answered and said unto her, O woman, great is thy faith: be it unto thee even as thou wilt. And

her daughter was made whole from that very
hour. (Matthew 15:22-28)

Christ did not seem interested at first and certainly
His disciples didn't seem to care, but she persistently
asked for her daughter to be healed. Our Lord seemed
to be testing her, for at the end he commended
her for her faith. In the words of Darby, she prayed
combatingly. She labored fervently. She wrestled. To
refer back to Moody's illustration, she didn't knock at
the door and run.

Apart from our prayer time, the daily reading of
the Scriptures is the other main part of a quiet time.
Any reading of the Bible has become easier in the time
in which we live due to electronic advances. Audible
books are now readily available to those who find their
visual ability too diminished to use. For those who can
read, but find it difficult to see the words, the ability to
adjust the size of numbers and letters is vital. Having a
backlight that you can brighten or dim is an enormous
help. When visual issues are severe, lighting and size of
font can make the difference between reading and not
reading. From a practical point of view, it is very easy
to avoid reading the Bible if you have to struggle to see
the words.

I believe that in the past at least two factors have
made me feel a certain sense of monotony with this
part of my time with God. Judging one's success at

Bible reading by the number of chapters read, rather than by how well one makes a personal application of those chapters, can lead to reading the Bible because of guilt rather than for a desire for God's leading and encouragement. Indeed, the volume of reading required in most reading plans makes absorption of the content nearly impossible in an ordinary schedule. Sometimes I stop after just a few verses because I am so blessed by what I've read that I need more time to absorb it and think about its application. Nor do I want to go on to something different until I've lived with what has blessed me and made it part of my life.

The other factor which can lead to a reluctance to read the Scriptures is feeling that one must always take an academic approach. The idea that unless you know Greek you'll never understand the New Testament is one example of the type of thinking which can make daily Bible reading seem hopeless and therefore boring. Some secondary sources of Greek can be a help in more extensive Bible study but not always in the shorter quiet time one has in order to live one's daily life. As Christians we need both daily fellowship and Bible reading with our Lord as well as periods of more intense Bible study. When the PURPOSE and METHOD of the reading are in sync, Bible reading is a lifeline for the Believer.

In the daily reading of the Bible, as one goes into the day it is fine to check a Greek word or two or to cross reference a concept. We should use our brains. But the basic purpose of daily Bible reading should guide us. When I read the Bible in that quiet time in the morning, before the rush of the day starts, my focus has become inspiration, guidance for the day and self evaluation – in other words, preparation for the day ahead of me. A broader scope of biblical knowledge is more the focus of intense Bible study which may be accompanied by a Bible study class with a teacher and, more privately, in personal study, combined with a good concordance, a Bible dictionary, several translations of the Bible and at least one trusted commentary.

One's daily devotional reading is more meditative in nature. Application and feelings are more involved. There is fellowship with God in both the time of prayer and the Bible reading. The day ahead is focused and fortified. We can go on.

Once again it is interesting to me how the surge in electronic thinking and development seem to refer back centuries to God Himself and ancient biblical verbiage. In John 16:23-24 (*TLB*) we read the words:

> At that time you won't need to ask me for anything, for you can go directly to the Father and ask him, and he will give you what you ask for because you use my name. You haven't tried this before, but begin now. Ask, using my name, and you will receive, and your cup of joy

will overflow.

In other words, because of Christ's redemptive work on the cross, we now have direct access to God. How? By presenting our "petitions over my [His] signature." (John 16:26, *TLB*). Reverently, the name of Jesus Christ becomes the divine password for our petitions to God the Father. That image can help our understanding. It is just as remarkable to consider having a cup of coffee with the God of all the Universe as it is to think of Christ's name as a divine password.

When I was in college, some leaders from IVCF tried to teach us students to engage in more casual prayer to ensure privacy from those around us. For example, two or three students eating apples while they prayed together looked like students who were just talking to each other, not praying. I was uncomfortable with that approach. It didn't seem reverent. Now I realize that such an approach can be used reverently if it is done properly,

When used with an attitude of reverence, modern terms like "password" can be consistent with biblical descriptions of God and His relationship to mankind: like God the Father or Christ our Shepherd, both references to earthly objects. Even more daring but biblical in origin is referring to God as the Bridegroom of the Church and looking back at the intimacy between God and mankind portrayed in the Song of

Solomon. God wants to be our Friend. He is indeed our Friend. But He is not the "man upstairs." He is God.

On that rainy Sunday when I couldn't get to church, my 20-minute prediction for prayer alone turned into much more, a full 45 minutes. When I finally looked at the clock my whole quiet time had lasted an hour and 15 minutes. It was a time I had learned to really enjoy, so much so that the "proverbial time flies" did indeed happen. Even though I hadn't thought of timing it before, I'm pretty sure my quiet time has been longer than it used to be and it is certainly more effective and more enjoyable. It is truly what having a cup of coffee with God implies. It has become a closer time with God, and as a result I am more appreciative of His holiness and power. My sense of His being truly God Almighty has increased, not diminished.

SEVEN

A Foxhole in My Mind

A number of years ago when a dear aunt of mine lay dying in a local hospital, she told me in clear definite words, "I am dying." At an earlier time she had said to me "I'm going to be with the Lord." The early words were uttered in a relaxed joyous way, as if she were content. Now she sounded more clinical as she talked about dying, more definite. As I talked to her physician, I knew she was probably accurate. He thought she wouldn't last the night. My emotions fought against this conclusion since she was the last remaining relative I had any contact with and we were very close.

Making the situation more complicated, during these last hours there had been added pressure from certain members of the medical profession to do more invasive tests, which even they agreed would not be of much help to the patient. Indeed, with her severe osteoporosis she would have ended up with broken ribs and even more pain than she was already experiencing.

"Do you want a 'no code'?" her doctor asked me. A "no code" would mean that if an emergency occurred, like breathing problems or heart failure, no heroics would be performed. Did I want to avoid any more extreme measures which would not prolong her life to any measurable degree but would cause a more painful death?

"I have to think," I replied. I'm so pro-life that my immediate response was to do even more to prolong my aunt's life, to test more and treat harder. Fortunately, I was granted time to make that difficult decision.

I left the hospital in search of a safe place to think and pray. I ended up at Bob's Big Boy restaurant, a lifelong safety zone of mine. Bob's went back to my years at Burbank High School. It was an afterschool hangout where my friends and I would talk, eat heavily salted French fries and drink cherry cokes. We complained about school, we made plans for college and we talked about dating and family issues. These are some of the types of things people do in a safety zone.

But what exactly is a safety zone? It is a place, a person, a belief, an activity which provides the opportunity for relief from stress, privacy for contemplation, an atmosphere in which to grieve, a place to rejoice, a chance to feel safe. We each have our safety zones which are unique to us. One man's safety zone may be another man's place of torture. A home can be a safety zone for some or a place of deep distress for someone else. The ocean is one of my favorite safety zones, but then again I've never watched a loved one drown.

My aunt Lydia and my family had been a safety zone for me since my birth, and now I was about to lose the only close remaining member of that family. But it was in my high school hangout, Bob's, that I was about to find my answer as to what to do regarding my aunt's illness, an answer given from my greatest safety zone of all, God.

As I entered Bob's, I automatically went back in my mind to my usual place of safety from way back in those high school days. As in those teenage years, a group of kids were close by, laughing, shouting and eating, just hanging out like we did. Without even thinking, I ordered the usual French fries and cherry coke. Then quietly I whispered a request to my Heavenly Father, "Please show me what's right."

As I blocked out the noise around me, the answer came. While clearly knowing, of course, that at any stage of dying God can heal, nevertheless generally, if the patient is in the actual dying process, to use dramatic testing and treatments which are declared unlikely to be effective to try to bring them back will often only prolong the dying process and increase the patient's suffering. My own personal word from God for all of this was: "You need to let her go. You cannot save her."

A peace flooded my being as I picked up my phone and called the doctor. After he heard my conclusion, he asked me to wait so I could speak to two nurses.

Then he said to me, "She's just now going into a code. If you can get back to the hospital fast enough, you can still see her one last time."

I was very close to the hospital, but it was night when I reached it and so the hospital guard started to stop me. When I explained, he urged me to hurry, but I was too late. The look on her face, however, reassured me that the decision had been right. She was with her Saviour, Jesus Christ.

Safety zones are not reserved for crisis times only nor are they always consciously created or even immediately recognizable as a safety zone. Some people have a favorite restaurant, for example, which serves food they aren't really fond of. But they like the people who run it or it's location by the beach, and so they always feel better when they go home after being there. They may often choose to go there without knowing why except that they leave feeling more relaxed or more motivated about a new project.

Sometimes one does know why a certain unlikely place lifts one up in a unique way. One man I knew used to love to have lunch at the worst-looking place in the neighborhood surrounding his workplace. When I asked him why he went there, he told me his story. For months he had been battling depression over the suicide of his oldest son. Some of the same suicidal thoughts had been playing around in his own mind in more recent weeks. One day in a fit of depression, not caring where or what he ate, he left his lunch friends and wandered into a dingy little coffee shop just to get away from the crowd, away from anyone he knew. Looking up over a counter filled with trinkets and candies for sale, he saw a small wooden sign with the words "Never, Never, Never Give Up" engraved on its surface. The words lifted him up. Death became something to run away from, especially self-inflicted death. The words on that simple piece of wood became a daily inspiration to live. Eventually, he no longer needed to actually see them. They were in his heart always. But at the beginning, those words, posted where all could see them, had made this little place his favorite restaurant, his special safety zone.

Some people seek to find a restaurant which always serves their favorite food, made to perfection. But in spite of all the outward perks, good food isn't always enough to make it a safety zone if the atmosphere is unpleasant and the people who run it are unfriendly. Consequently, in spite of the good food, chances are many people eventually quit going there and find a place where they feel happier after dining.

The first restaurant with the mediocre food can become a better safety zone for some simply because it makes them feel better in spite of the food. A lot of people feel better for having been there.

Safety zones are often simply discovered. We feel safe with a new friend. We feel uplifted when we hear a new song. We are refreshed by time spent alone in prayer and Bible reading in the morning, especially when we discover something we never noticed before. These experiences can become safety zones which we seek out repeatedly once we've discovered them.

Sometimes we do actually create a safety zone. I remember staying at a stranger's home during a church convention. The lady at whose home I stayed always kept a guest room available, just in case. Combined with her warm personality and her love of God, the room had a feeling of joy to start with. Then there was the attractiveness and thoughtfulness in how the room was set up. Fresh flowers in a vase, along with a crystal carafe of water, had been placed on the bed table. The sheets were light blue and scented with lavender. A nearby crystal lamp along with a small stand of books finished off the accessories of the room, while a small set of drawers and a rocking chair completed the more practical necessities. Wall decorations and calming colors of paint and carpeting finished the scene. The lady was a widow in her upper years who chose to serve the church with her God-given gift of hospitality. For the tired stranger in their midst she created a safety zone along the way.

Caves and secret places have always held an appeal to children. In the hills above the house where I grew up there was a cave, allegedly a bear cave, which all of us kids on the street below knew about but were too scared to explore. We opted out by trying to dig a hole to China, and when that didn't work we settled for pitching a small tent in the backyard.

Sometimes even in adulthood we seek our private, even secret, place and it too becomes our safety zone. During the closing months of World War II, after he had been catapulted into the presidency following the death of Franklin Roosevelt, Harry Truman was asked how he handled the tremendous pressures which had been laid upon him by these events. His answer was: "I have a foxhole in my mind …" He further explained that just as a soldier escapes from danger by retreating into his foxhole for protection, he had a private place in his mind which afforded him a sense of respite and protection, a foxhole in his mind. We each have many such foxholes, safety zones which are readily available the instant we need them, foxholes in our mind.

Memories can destroy us or they can be an encouraging safety zone. We choose which it will be. Within a short span of eight years, I lost my mother, father, two aunts, and two uncles by death plus my sister and her family of five in a different, more painful way. My memories ranged from deep grief and loss to a bitter facing of reality with regard to my sister.

But out of the darkness emerged the safety zone of a different set of memories: Christmas Eve, Swedish style, with all my family who had just died but who came to life again in those memories, became a safety zone of comfort and made Christmas better for the memories rather than a time of grief. Fishing with my father off the Malibu Pier when I was a child, learning to cook with my mother, learning bits of Chinese words and numbers as well as something about Chinese cooking from my aunt Ruth: all of these provided pleasant memories of comfort. The list seems endless. But it was my choice as to which memories I played, negative or positive. The positive became safety zones.

Another foxhole in the mind which can become a safety zone is found in aspirations. In his poem "Rabbi Ben Ezra," Robert Browning wrote in part:

> All I could never be,
>   All men ignored in me
> This, I was worth to God, whose wheel the pitcher
>   Shaped.[1]

And, consistent with the concept of the safety zone of aspiration, Browning adds:

> What I aspired to be,
> And was not, comforts me.[2]

In 1949, when Walter Annenberg found himself seated next to Winston Churchill at a formal dinner, he turned to Churchill and expressed his regrets over Churchill's defeat in the previous election after his great service to the country during World War II. Churchill's reply was: "Young Annenberg, look not for rewards from others but hope you have done your best." To know you have done your best, to even aspire to do your best, these provide genuine safety zones in your mind which are healing to all the defeat and failure which are an inevitable part of life.

Ultimately God is our greatest safety zone and with that fact comes the challenge to spend time with Him. No matter what goes wrong in our lives, He is there for us. His constant presence doesn't mean that He says "yes" to every request or that He instantly removes all pain. He does what is consistent with His will for our life. To have that assurance from our Creator, our Savior Who died for us on the cross, that by acceptance of Him we might spend eternity with Him, is by far the greatest safety zone available to mankind.

Issuing forth from our relationship with God come many new practical approaches to safety zones. A whispered cry for help from God as a crisis hits; meditation on a favorite Psalm as we're trying to go to sleep at night; a brief focus on a piece of scripture as God brings it to our mind during an argument: these are just a few potential safety zones available to each of us. A whispered "Thy love" in a moment of anger can utilize divine power and also provide the relief of a safety zone. Indeed the potential for safety zones within our relationship to God is endless.

One thing I have learned from life itself and from my conversations with people in my position as a psychotherapist is that life offers all of us times of pain, loneliness, and even hopelessness. Yet God is there for all of these, ready to help. When my family was taken from earth, some physical problems also complicated my situation. Yes, I felt lonely.

But then there was God and His resources. One of the most effective of those God-given resources was my deep sense of meaning. I was here by God's calling and neither I nor God was finished with my earthly life. Finishing well was something I owed to God, to myself, and to my parents. Once again, as has happened so often in my life, a poem came to mind which expressed my feelings so well. The last part reads:

> The woods are lovely, dark and deep.
> But I have promises to keep,
> And miles to go before I sleep,
> And miles to go before I sleep.
>   – Robert Frost

Those words have never left me! They too are a safety zone.

EIGHT

The Rock

"I have my rock back," the lady said to me with a smile of joy. It was a chance encounter at a random social event with a woman who had come to me for therapy a few years back. After counseling her and her husband for a couple of years, their marital problems had seemed to greatly improve. At least that was how I perceived things to be when we all agreed that the improvement was great enough to quit therapy. But one can rarely be one hundred per cent sure.

To have a partner who is your rock means that they share responsibilities in practical ways, which could include everything from finances and physical upkeep of the home to child rearing and support in many of the emotional ups and downs of life. No human being can meet all needs for another, but humanly speaking a sense of general support from one's spouse can make life a lot easier. Furthermore, to be someone's rock involves more than just physical support. It means encouraging and caring about that person as well as an occasional pointing out of a better way. The intensity to which this role might be present in a marriage is of course greater than that of a friendship and different from a child-parent relationship or that of close friends and business partnerships. Yet to be in some way a rock for someone is basic to any close relationship. It simply means you are someone who is there for them when they need you, someone who is strong when they are feeling weak.

Yet an earthly rock is still affected by the vicissitudes of life, which is why to know God as our ultimate Rock can make a profound difference in our lives. There is no predictable, permanent earthly rock. The refrain of an old hymn, written in the early 1800s by Edward Mote, says it well:

> On Christ, the solid Rock, I stand;
> All other ground is sinking sand.

There are many scriptural references to God as our Rock. "The Lord is my rock, and my fortress, and my deliverer; my God, my strength, in whom I will trust; my shield, and the horn of my salvation, and my high tower." (Psalm 18:2)

In Psalm 78:35 we read, "And they remembered that God was their rock, and the high God their redeemer."

In Psalm 31:1-3 we see the breadth of all that is included for us in Christ our Rock:

> In thee, O Lord, do I put my trust; let
> me never be ashamed. Deliver me in thy

righteousness.
Bow down thine ear to me; deliver me
speedily. Be thou my strong rock, for an
house of defense to save me.
For thou art my rock and my fortress;
therefore, for thy name's sake lead me, and
guide me.

The end result of this connection with God as the
Rock is summarized well in Isaiah 26:3-4:

> Thou wilt keep him in perfect peace,
> whose mind is stayed on thee, because he
> trusteth in thee.
> Trust ye in the Lord forever; for in the
> Lord God is everlasting strength.

Psalm 18:31 clearly states the position of God as our
Rock. Yet there are some who would take that position
away, and have done so early in church history. In
Matthew 16 Christ questions his disciple Peter about
who people say that He is. When it comes down to who
do YOU say I am, Peter answers: "Thou art the Christ,
the Son of the Living God." Then verse 18 clarifies for
all of eternity the identity of the Rock spoken of in the
Scriptures. When Peter is referred to as the rock, the
Greek word *petros* is used, literally "little rock," perhaps
a piece broken off from a larger rock. Whereas when

Christ is being referred to, the Greek word used is *petra* and thus identifies Christ as the One upon whom the Church is built. *Petra* is a large rock and is certainly what is being referred to when Christ goes on to say that His church will be built upon this Rock. Christ IS that Rock, not Peter as some teach.

As I was growing up, our family vacations were usually spent at a motel in Pacific Grove, California, called Butterfly Trees Lodge. It was located about 45 minutes from San Francisco and 10 minutes away from the center of Carmel by the Sea. There was plenty to do in all directions. Furthermore this motel was on the exact spot where many monarch butterflies migrated every year. At that time of year the trees were orange with the covering of monarchs.

Outside of the motel was a dirt road which curved to the right and led down to the coastline. On the way, to the right of the road, was a very old cemetery with gravestones dating back one or two hundred years. Then to the immediate left of the road was Point Pinos Lighthouse, which today is still in operation. As one reached the coast there was the ocean in all of its magnificence, surrounded by rocks of all sizes. Early on I spotted "my rock." It was a large, flattish rock a short way out from the shore, easily reachable by walking over a trail of smaller rocks. Its depth reached down into the ocean and it was firmly attached to the ocean floor. The water reached high enough to touch the rock but I don't remember it ever flooding the rock.

With Bible and perhaps other books in hand I would climb out on to the rock, get comfortable on its flattish surface and think and read and pray. What did God want me to do with my life: to be a physician, a missionary to China, like my Aunt Ruth whom I adored? Or was I to start an orphanage in China or a school anywhere? "Please God," I would plead, "let me do one of these." Ultimately the answer was "No!" Chronic Fatigue Syndrome made that answer final. (See my book *I'll Be Better in the Morning*.) I was not strong enough physically.

As we have seen in the Scriptures, Christ is clearly the Rock of our salvation. But He is also our Rock in our daily life, our refuge, our Guide, our sustenance. My rock in the coastal waters of Pacific Grove was just a rock, not even really my rock. But it was there, separate from the earth, and it became for me a place to seek God. It was safe and accessible. It was in an atmosphere I love, the ocean. On this earth God gives these things and many more to us so that we can use them to know Him better and follow His plan for us. He is our Rock, our Real Rock. My rock in northern California is just a mock-up of the Real. But God used it as an image of the Real.

Christ is our Rock in everyday practical living. Years ago I learned a hymn which had the refrain, "Christ liveth in me." It was in the old Keswick hymn book

and taught to me at the Christian private high school
I attended. Later in reading from the writings of A. B.
Simpson, I saw the full meaning of what it means to
literally allow Christ to live His life out through us, to
be our Rock in the problems of life.

In his twenties Dr. Simpson developed a debilitating
heart problem which made his ministry very difficult.

Usually it took him until Wednesday to get over
the effects of his Sunday sermons. Climbing stairs or
even a slight elevation was suffocating agony.

>Dr. Simpson was only thirty-seven when
>he was told by his physician that he might
>not have long to live. On his doctor's advice,
>he went for a long rest to the resort town of
>Old Orchard Beach, Maine. There he happened
>into an unusual religious meeting conducted
>by a Boston physician, Dr. Charles Cullis. Dr.
>Cullis was then having much success with
>treating tubercular patients through prayer and
>common sense health measures alone.
>
>Several statements made in the meeting
>about healing through prayer sent Dr. Simpson
>back to the Bible to find out what Jesus had to
>say on the subject. He soon became convinced
>that Jesus had always meant for His gospel to
>include healing of the body along with healing
>of the mind and the spirit.

In the quiet of his room, Dr. Simpson reviewed his life. He was always struggling desperately for even his minimal needs – for enough health to keep going, for enough ideas and intellectual resources to write talks and sermons, for enough caring about other people. It was almost as if his creed was "Of myself I must do everything." But somehow he always fell short of his objectives. Was God now trying to reach him with a new idea? Had he ever really given God a chance to run his life?

One Friday afternoon shortly after that, Dr. Simpson went for a walk. Since he was always out of breath, he was forced to walk slowly. The path led into a pine wood, and he sat down on a fallen log to rest. All around him was that thick carpet of moss so often seen in the Maine woods. Sunlight filtered through the tall pines, laying striped patterns across the emerald green floor. Simpson pulled out his watch and saw that it was three o'clock.

"All things in my life looked dark and withered," Simpson wrote afterward. "The doctors had made it clear that they could do nothing for me. Intellectual life and spiritual life were also at a low ebb. So there in the woods I asked God to become my life for me, including physical life for all the needs of my body until my life work was done. And I solemnly promised to use His spiritual and physical strength in me for the good of others. God was there all right, because every fiber of my body was tingling with His Presence. He had come to meet me at the point of my helplessness."

A few days later, Simpson took a long hike and climbed a mountain three thousand feet high. "When I reached the mountaintop," he related joyously, "the world of weakness and fear was lying at my feet. From that time I literally had a new heart in my breast."[1]

After this experience Simpson lived a vigorous life, wrote and preached continually, and died at the age of 76.

God uses many things on this earth to sustain and guide us. The communion service is an opportunity to see what God has done for us and in us and provides a particularly sacred form of worship. The Bible, godly sermons and Bible studies, and hymns are all vehicles for knowing this real Rock of our life better so that in earthly life He is truly our Rock, not only in eternity. He is our Saviour, our Guide, our Sustenance, our Hope, our Father, our Comforter, our ALL. He is indeed our ROCK. And sometimes He works through earthly rocks like other Christians or even other creations made by Him, like my rock in the ocean up north or another scene of nature. But He Himself is the only reliable rock. The hymn has it right in the words "All other ground is sinking sand."

Once we realize that Christ is our Rock, our ultimate question is how to have access to that Rock and put what we learn into practice. Two simple words can answer that question: "By Faith."

As a psychotherapist who wants to help people, I have always liked most of the people I work with. In my job it certainly helps to like people. Once in a rare while there are exceptions, however. Angry, bossy, controlling women can be one of those, but usually I can rather quickly get rid of any negativity. One woman, however, stands out in my mind. I could readily understand why she had conflicts with every member of her family and had few friends. I recognized the problem rather quickly, but managed to remain personally unaffected by it at first. Then gradually I began to feel better about my day on those occasions when she came late or even canceled her session. Her late payments annoyed me further and I began to be a clock watcher.

One day right before our appointment I faced my feelings. I just didn't want to see her anymore, even though she seemed happy enough about the sessions and had kept coming. I had about ten minutes left before she would arrive. I began to silently pray: "Lord, I can't stand this woman. Help me to feel differently about her." Pause. "Lord, I still don't like her. I want to quit." Silence. Deafening silence. Then suddenly I prayed differently, as if God was gently telling me He had come into my life years ago and now He would live His life out through me if I let Him. "Lord," I prayed once again. "I can't do this. I can't even like her, much less love her, but I take your love, your caring, and I give my dislike to you. I can't do this on my own," I whispered as she walked in the door.

As she came in and sat down, there flooded over me a whole new feeling. Once again I wanted to help her. I saw the potential for growth I usually see in people. I cared. For a number of months my positive feelings were tested at times, but they never left. On the day of our last appointment, we both knew she had become a very different person, someone who had friends and a much happier family. I had cared. God had worked through me because now I had appropriated His power in and through me. During the course of her therapy, whenever I had felt any of those old negative feelings, I could always turn to God and whisper "Thy love, Lord. Thy love." And it came. "We take, He undertakes." We conquer by faith, not by trying to feel love or joy by our own efforts, but by faith TAKING them from God Who holds them out to us on open hands to be taken by faith.

As a very small child, I went with my parents to a large church in Los Angeles, the Church of the Open

Door. All these years later I still remember one phrase that the pastor, J. Vernon McGee, used repeatedly regarding Scripture: "Put it into shoe leather." To take all of the promises of God and to access the ability to keep his commandments is to put God's word into shoe leather. We just take and go forward believing.

One of the most dramatic examples of this truth in this century occurred in the life of evangelist Billy Graham a short time before his first major crusade, the "1949 Tent Crusade" in Los Angeles. I was a Christian before that crusade but I remember being there with my parents and being at many more crusades throughout the years. They deeply influenced my life.

Henrietta Mears was influential in that first crusade. She was also in my life when I was still a child and went to Sunday school at the First Presbyterian Church in Hollywood. It was a Sunday school which Miss Mears had totally changed with her written material. We didn't play a lot in Sunday school; we studied the Bible. I remember Miss Mears as an awesome lady with incredible hats. Huge, decorated hats.

A few weeks before the Los Angeles Crusade, Miss Mears invited Graham to speak at Forest Home. At that time Graham was having some conflicts within himself over the veracity of the Scriptures. It was an untimely experience for him, coming as it did right before the Crusade which was to be the start of a lifetime of preaching to huge groups of people.

One evening a few weeks before the Crusade started, Graham went up into the San Bernardino Mountains behind Forest Home to pray. Confronting his doubts, he prayed: "Father, I am going to accept this as thy Word – by faith!" Relief poured over his being and his faith increased and sustained him the rest of his life. After that night he felt a deeper relationship with God than he had ever known before. By faith he had stood on the Rock and had been held secure.

> On Christ, the solid Rock, I stand;
> All other ground is sinking sand.

NINE

Red Ribbons

Psalm 119:105 reads: "Thy word is a lamp unto my feet, and a light unto my path." When I think of a lamp unto my feet I think of being sure of my next move, or I imagine safety measures like avoiding objects which could make me stumble. On the other hand, when I imagine a lighted path I think more long term like my end goal and finding the right direction to take. God has given us the Bible as a map, a guidebook, for every moment of our life's journey.

In Psalm 119:11 we read: "Thy word have I hid in mine heart, that I might not sin against thee." Notice that WE hide His word in our hearts. This is why we need daily devotional time with God, group Bible studies, church meetings and sermons, and a host of other ways to help us maintain the word of God in our thinking. Then in a crisis, and on the most ordinary day in our life, the Holy Spirit Who indwells us as Believers can bring thoughts or actual words from His Word, which may be hidden in our subconscious, to our consciousness and then enable us to live each day with God's specific leading and encouragement.

The famous poet Henry Wadsworth Longfellow

once wrote the words:

> Into each life some rain must fall,
> Some days must be dark and dreary.

We all have some of these days, and it is often on such days that I have found God gives His special words of hope, for ourselves and at times for others. I may wake up, for example, feeling gloomy about a given day and then words like "The joy of the Lord is your strength" come into my mind and fill me with a more positive feeling about the day, even at times a joy of anticipation. Some days remain gray, but maybe not quite as gray as they first felt. Not all days are the same. But with God lifting us up through His Word they become possible and many times full of His joy and peace. It is at this point of discovery that it becomes part of our work for God to reach out to others when God shares a word or thought with us which seems to fit the circumstances which someone else is enduring.

About a year ago, a friend of mine was close to death. His wife, a nurse, was very faithful in her care of him. As I woke up one morning, a Bible verse came to my mind which encouraged me. Then I felt a strong prompting to share that thought with her. So I messaged the verse: "I will help thee." And I went on to add, "This blessed me this morning as I read in Charles Spurgeon's daily reading … thought it might bless you."

She wrote back: "… I needed that. Was up most of the night trying to get him comfortable." My friend's death came a short time later.

Then, right before Christmas, once again I felt led to share with his wife. "Thinking about you as we get into Christmas. The words, 'As your days so shall your strength be,' came to me as I wrote this. You are loved."

The next day she wrote back, "Your timing is amazing. Was just pondering my life." My timing was not the real issue. On both occasions God brought the verse to mind and then again the thought of whom to send it to. But it was important to have some Bible verses for Him to draw from.

When I was around eight years of age, my parents decided to move our family from a very excellent church to the First Presbyterian Church in Hollywood. Some criticized that move but it was one of the best decisions my parents ever made in terms of its effect on me. And it was a very unselfish move since they made it primarily because of the Sunday school. It was during the days when Henrietta Mears had a great influence on the Sunday school at that church. Gospel Light Press was publishing excellent and even challenging Sunday school curriculum. And the staff at church were well chosen. Above all was their approach to memorization. Each student was given a choice of memory verses. These were not just simple verses, but many times it involved whole passages, like John 15, or Romans 8, or a Psalm. Each time we completed a memory piece, we would recite it to our Sunday School teacher. She would give us a paper cutout with a shape related to the verse. For example, for Psalm 23 the cutout would relate to sheep. The Ten Commandments had the look of a scroll. Each time we successfully recited a verse and were given our cutout, it was attached to our own red ribbon, a ribbon which extended from the ceiling to the floor and beyond. The students started competing to have the longest ribbon. It began to be a problem when there was not enough time for all of us to recite these verses to our teacher each week, so our teacher, Miss Stevens, allowed some of us to recite them over the phone during the week.

I still have that red ribbon today, many years later. And in the oddest way, when I think I've forgotten those verses, they burst into my memory just when I need them. It's the same with other verses learned in other ways, like verses my parents quoted a lot, or favorites of my missionary aunt, Ruth Benson, or verses I've just memorized through the years. They provide a storehouse of help in all sorts of life situations, offering guidance and encouragement for myself and others I may be trying to help. And always there is that basic storage of knowledge from those years in Sunday School back at Hollywood Presbyterian Church. I will never forget that red ribbon, and the kind Miss Stevens who cared enough to allow us to recite those extra verses by phone.

The red ribbon example is something for all of us to think about as we work with children. In those younger years children need props in order to motivate them and to help them remember. Pictures or symbols like those on the ribbons help in learning and even small rewards can motivate. A reward of an ice cream sundae may offend some Christians who feel that a child should study the Scriptures without any outside motivation. But if through that ice cream reward a child memorizes a verse, as life goes on the verse itself will come to mean far more than any other reward. It will be its own reward. And that's our goal, isn't it? A teacher who cares, without shaming or dominating, can encourage a child to learn about God.

To become a Christian is simple but yet profound at any age. It involves accepting Christ's sacrifice on the cross as payment for our sin and inviting Him to come and live in our lives. We accept Him as Lord and Saviour. John 3:16 still says it best. Then with Christ living His life out through us by the power of the Holy Spirit, fueled by a store of knowledge of His word, the Bible, we are enabled to grow in our Christian life and reach out effectively and lovingly to others. Based on Galatians 2:20, an old hymn says it well:

> Christ liveth in me,
> Christ liveth in me,

Oh! what a salvation this,
That Christ liveth in me.

As Christians we are to be living examples of Christ in us living His life out through us. After the death of evangelist Billy Graham, I had occasion to communicate with the Billy Graham Library and the BGEA offices several times. One thing struck me: everyone who operated those phones reflected the love of Christ in their tone of voice and in their general handling of the subject I called about. To me that was a striking example of Christ living His life out through His followers. If I had not been a Christian, I would have wanted to know more about becoming one after encountering these people. The Bible challenges us to be this way – indeed it commands us. It is the end result of a Spirit-filled life fueled by biblical truth.

Since the results of biblical input are lifelong, the input must go beyond the boundaries of childhood. A daily quiet time with God is vital to all Christian growth as are group Bible studies and sermons. Furthermore, now and then interactions with some of the giants of Christian faith can offer an incredible influence, even if they're long gone and we only have their books.

At the outset of my writing Christian books, two men, both pastors, offered unique wisdom in certain areas of my writing. When I was writing in areas which involved a lot about theology, I would often turn to

Ken Connolly, a Baptist preacher with an unusual background in theological subjects. John Whorrall, who was the pastor of University Bible Church in Westwood, California, was a great help in church history. Both are now with the Lord, and I still miss their wisdom, encouragement and friendship.

All through my life I seem to have had such help. A.J. Crick was a British scholar and was part of the open group of Plymouth Brethren. Periodically when I was in college, he used to come to the United States to hold meetings. He would speak once or usually twice on Sunday and then nightly, Monday through Friday, while he was here. Usually my boyfriend and I taped his messages and could share some of them afterwards. So many people like these have blessed my life in this way: Dr. Marchant King's seminary class on theology and Dr. Grace King's Sunday afternoon Bible classes on the Old Testament, along with classes by other teachers and pastors.

It is important that our Bible study become integrated with our lives. As we learn more about God through His word, let us not forget to love others more because of what we learn. Sometimes we Christians tend to turn people off because of our rigidity.

In contrast to that, a few years ago, after I had missed church for several weeks because of illness, the rector of our church came to visit and encourage. He brought with him the articles needed for Holy Communion.

The next Sunday was Christmas Sunday. "I couldn't take the chance of your missing this on Christmas Sunday," he said with a smile. He knew how much I looked forward to that weekly sacrament. We took it together, with his leading on the reading because of some trouble I was having with my eyes. It was a short but meaningful few minutes, but the kindness involved with this act, during a very busy part of the year for him, touched me deeply. I will remember it as a simple but unique act of truly Christian behavior. This is what Christ living in me should look like to the world. This is what Bible study should lead to.

> Thy word have I hid in mine heart,
> that I might not sin against thee.
> > (Psalms 119:11)

TEN

Sometimes It's the Simple Things That Matter

It was a pleasant day in January. My granddaughter's birthday was in the next few days, but my daughter and I wanted to wait until Libby's father got home to celebrate. That made today the perfect day for girls' lunch out. We ended up at a restaurant we had gone to a number of times in the past. But I had never looked at the whole menu before, at least not at the dessert section. There it was on the menu: C.C. Brown Hot Fudge Sundae. But it couldn't be, I thought. None of us had planned on having dessert after a rather heavy lunch, but now we had to – at least I had to. We ordered sundaes and my mind went back to a place and time long ago.

I was back in an ice cream parlor on Hollywood Boulevard in a different Hollywood from today. The sundaes were served in fluted glass dishes: ice cream topped with whipped cream and a sprinkle of finely chopped nuts. To the side of each dish was an individual serving of hot fudge sauce, properly warm, in a small silver pitcher. It was fun and the sundae was delicious. But for me it was something different still. It was a vivid memory come to life once again of a past family happening, a Saturday night treat that my parents and I frequently enjoyed when I was still a small child. My parents have been gone for years, but this memory stands out in my mind and comforts.

When I was a little older, my mother and father and I built another routine into our lives together, Saturday night swimming at the Pasadena YWCA. Afterwards we would go home and go sleepily to bed. But it was fun at any age and I learned a lot about swimming from my once lifeguard, then engineer, father.

Learning how to cook by spending time with my mother in the kitchen, particularly before a holiday like Christmas, was another happy and predictable time of my growing up. No boxed mixes – all the baked goods were made "from scratch," as we called it. Just the real thing. Between my mother's Swedish recipes and the next-door neighbor's German supply of the same, Christmas arrived with multiple varieties of decorated cookies. I learned a lot about cooking, and the experience had been fun.

Another happy tradition remains with me from early childhood, right as World War II was ending. My father, who was an engineer at Lockheed, would come home from work at unexpected times. Sometimes his irregular hours caused anxiety for his family at home, so my parents would try to create happy times when he arrived. This was important during a time when national stress was still high. There was fear of enemy submarines in the California coastal waters, and fear of bombers overhead, all left over anxiety from the war which lingered for a while even when it had officially ended. There were memories, too, of war scenes from movies, newsreels, and photos. Among these were atrocities to certain groups of people, like the Jews; war scenes with children crying and cities destroyed. The process of recovery took time and was greatly helped by close family and friend connections as well as simple pleasures. Simplicity was the rule of the day.

During this early period of recovery from war, on nights when my father came home especially late, I would try to stay awake even though I was in bed. My father would peek into the room where my sister and I slept, and we would immediately let him know we were awake. In minutes we had our outdoor coats on over our pajamas. Sleepy but happy, we got into the car with our parents. Our destination? Bob's Big Boy, a local restaurant which was a favorite of many families and an afterschool hangout for the majority of local kids. Sitting in the car in the drive-in section of the restaurant, we enjoyed a midnight snack. Life felt normal again and safe.

There were so many times like this in my childhood, so much of life which did not involve electronic devices or established activities like competitive sports. I could throw a ball through a basketball hoop my Dad had attached to the garage and just enjoy and use the time to think. I could experiment with a new recipe and not worry about my mother's rejection if it failed. When I was really young, I could enjoy making mud pies in our back yard and come back in the house all muddy without my mother getting angry. She just filled the tub with warm water and bubble bath.

My sister and I were blessed in having parents who made their own mistakes but didn't cripple us by making the mistake of trying to live their lives out through us. Rather, they encouraged us to pursue our own goals. While they were exacting in areas of honesty and manners, they did not hover over us trying to make us the football champion they never became or the glamour queen of the senior prom.

Adults, however, were not free from the stress of war, along with the stress of a new period of history which, for many, involved life changes. For example, many women started going to work outside of the home. This occurred during the war to help sustain the war effort and often became a way of life afterwards. A little more money, a better house, became motivations, as well as college expenses for a new generation who now needed that education in order to obtain more lucrative and at times more fulfilling careers. Each change brought another. Men needed to assume more household tasks, as did older children. There was often less time for simple pleasures.

As a result of the changes in roles within a family unit, other changes and demands occurred. Prepared foods began to be sold in the market with a dubious effect on entertaining and even health, but they did give a break to the working woman. With increased pressure on the adults and older children in a family, the need for positive outlets became even more vital. My parents found a release in their artwork. My mother painted seascapes and other landscape scenes in oil and pen and ink. My father tended to use watercolor and often included buildings and ships in the objects he chose to portray. The artwork increased their friendships with people of like interests and helped them forget some of the past horrors of war. They were adults with their own needs, not just parents. The new focus was good for all involved.

No one, past or present, has ever grown up in the perfect environment. Indeed any generation faces its own challenges and difficulties. Today's parents face increased demands with less leisure time or outlets. One of the biggest challenges today lies in living in the emergence of an electronic age, which can help in saving time while it also creates its own use of time and stress. I am writing today on my iPad; this morning I scheduled an appointment with a client using my iPhone; last night I searched on my Macbook for a poem I had written a long time ago. Yes, we are connected to our electronic devices, but they can only be valuable if we control them rather than their controlling us. On this particular morning these devices were a help, even a time saver. But such is not always true.

A while back a five-year-old child walked into my office proudly waving his iPhone. "I'm not supposed to call anyone," he said to me. "We got it for him because we don't want him to feel deprived," his mother explained as she walked in behind him. "Deprived?" I thought. What a dumb reason to buy an inappropriate item for a child.

The other day I was tired of thinking and tired in general, so I turned on my computer and searched to see if I could find the movie *The Sound of Music*. I spent the rest of the afternoon watching it and felt pleasantly refreshed. I was too tired to have gone to a theater and couldn't have found that particular movie at that particular time anyway. It was a good use of technology. It provided a simple pleasure like that hot fudge sundae years ago. And there are many other good uses: writing letters, research, communicating with friends and general communication for business, buying and selling, and so on. But it can also be a destroyer of simple pleasures and creates its own stress. When a group of friends or family sit in a room having a conversation, and a few people space off from the group and read or text on their mobile phone, comprehension of the conversation around them as well as manners go down the proverbial drain. On the contrary, when children are brought up to view such behavior as rude, hopefully they will handle their social use of electronic devices responsibly.

Each of us can find what we want on the Internet. There are different levels of accuracy and bias for the reporting of news. Biblical truth can be taught accurately and be uplifting or it can be misinterpreted. Medical tests can be checked, jobs searched and classes taken.

But some subjects like sex can also be exploited and, often along with images of violence, become a major source of harmful entertainment, like pornography. The Internet can be helpful or destructive – and children, and even adults, need training to understand it better and use it for God's glory. So far it seems to be overly influential in its negative effect. Yet my movie-watching that day restored me because it was relaxing and positive. For young children there should be adult supervision as to what they watch to make this a safe way to go. That too takes time. A tablet left unsupervised is not a good babysitter, especially when placed with a baby in a crib. Use a picture book instead or, better still, interact and read a story!

One of the greatest problems which parents with teenagers present during my counseling sessions with them is the constant use of video games, particularly an issue between older children and their parents. One time when I was talking with a teenage boy he told me about the games he played online. I had to admit I had never played a video game. He handed me his device and said "Try it." I did. The game focused around a military scene with soldiers ducking in and out of shacks in an area which seemed to have turned into a battlefield. "Shoot at them when they come toward you. Or they'll shoot you," the boy said. "OK" I replied, but I was determined to let them shoot first. Really getting into it, I wasn't willing to shoot first.

Looking at the bottom of the screen, I saw a heap of something. "What's that?" I asked the boy as I pointed toward it. "Your blood," he answered. "They shot you." I suddenly became angry. "I'll get them," I muttered. A few shots later the boy shouted, "Hey, stop, you've won." "How can I have won?" I asked. "I just started." But the numbers were there. I had indeed won.

The boy looked at me admiringly and respected my aim. I felt like a killer. I had a glimmer of how destructive these imaginary games could be. A lot of what is encountered on the Internet is negative. Handing it over to kids is in many ways dangerous without some solid instruction. Furthermore, the time used, if excessive, takes children away from a swim with a big brother or a cup of hot chocolate with a parent. It takes away from the little time left in this busy world for simple pleasures.

Children are not unique in needing restrictions regarding their use of the Internet. It is far too easy to access pornography and/or find a sex partner or drug contacts online. Adults need to self-restrict in these areas as they must in other addictive areas. For the Christian, it is vital to spend daily time with the Lord if one is to responsibly handle the problems inherent in modern day technology. Direct accountability to God through confession and prayer greatly raises one's sense of responsibility, and knowing we face Him daily in that way is a big motivation for responsible living. Additionally, the saturation with the Bible in that time of our daily "cup of coffee with God" increases our desire and our ability to obey Him. Church attendance, group Bible study, and other similar activities all add to our ability to live in a way which honors God.

Electronic equipment and the Internet are just the latest advances in our modern life. Like the car, which brought us out of the horse and buggy age into greater speed in transportation, every major introduction to our lifestyle brings its own hazards. The thought of atomic power, for example, brings terror to our minds. Most of us just block that thought from our thinking. But in our daily life we can do things which make a difference. The red ribbon back in my Sunday school days, for example, helped me look forward to going to church every Sunday morning as a child. I learned early to find joy in small things, like that Saturday night swim or hot fudge sundaes, which involved close family outings, not just food. The need for simple things which buffer some of the larger negative events in life holds true for any age, adult as well as childhood.

Some people I know look for comfort and friendship in social networking, and sometimes there are real relationships built that way. But you can't have dinner with most of your online friends or even encounter them. I have several I value a lot and wish they lived nearby. But too often we don't really know each other and never meet. The worst possibility is that some people retreat and actually like to have distant friends because they feel safe with that distance. There's less likelihood of being hurt by those who never really know you, but there is also less likelihood of being helped.

The hot fudge sundae treat to look forward to at the end of the week, along with the sharing in conversation that was involved, is an example of experiencing closeness with others, family or friends, in a small event which also helps in its anticipation. Be it small or large, something to share or look forward to can be uplifting at all ages. In the same way, at five or one hundred and five, a loving good night at the end of a day is still welcome, a brief phone conversation with someone who understands can create a good night's sleep. And we can do better than even that in providing variation and special moments of sometimes unexpected joy as well as planned times of happiness for ourselves and others. Life doesn't have to be quite as complicated as we sometimes make it. Sometimes it's the simple things that matter.

ELEVEN

In Jesus' Name

The last time I went to have my hair cut I was not prepared for yet a new technological surprise. As my credit card was being processed, I was asked for my PIN number. PIN, password? Who carries those around in their head? Some do, I guess. I had never been asked for either before, except when I was buying online at home and could look them up in my little green book where I keep them. Furthermore, online it's usually the password that is asked for. I wouldn't have known that either without my password book. My granddaughter paid. Passwords have become important in our society.

Because of my severe mobility problems due to osteoarthritis, it is sometimes hard for me to do public speaking which involves a lot of travel or engagements which require long and usually multiple sessions. Partly as a result I have felt led into a greater focus on prayer as a part of my calling from God.

Lately I have been reading in the book of Acts for part of my morning quiet time. Sometimes a concept or one word will jump out at me as I read. This time it was in Acts 4:30 as the whole early church joined in prayer to the Lord with Peter and John. In verse 30 we read: "… send your healing power, and may miracles and wonders be done by the name of your holy servant Jesus." This verse reminded me that as children we were always taught to add "in Jesus' name" at the end of every prayer. Also, as adults we still often end our prayers with those same words.

When Christ was on this earth, if He was walking along a road, He often stopped to meet human needs, like healing. But in this chapter He has ascended up to Heaven. He is no longer here in physical form. But performing miracles are still done in His Name.

Nor is the purpose of praying in Jesus' name limited to healing. Looking at the multitude of Bible references to praying in Jesus' name, the purpose of so doing is to use the power of that name and the redemptive work it represents. It is our way of access to the Lord. Up to this time Christ had been on earth, accessible to those who encountered Him physically along the road. He was and still is, through His Name, the "one mediator between God and men." Now, by the power of the Holy Spirit, the risen Christ lives in us who belong to Him and by His name we have instant access to the Father. We can pray with the authority of That name, JESUS! The name of Jesus becomes our password to God.

And whatsoever ye shall ask the Father in my name, that will I do … If ye ask any thing in my name, I will do it. I have chosen you … that whatever ye ask of the Father in my name, he may give it unto you. Verily, verily, I say unto you, Whatever ye shall ask the Father in my name, he will give you. Until now ye have asked nothing in my name: ask, and ye shall receive, that your joy may be fulfilled. In that day ye shall ask in my name. – John 14:13-14; 15:16; 16:23-24, 26

In my name – repeated six times. Our Lord knew how slow our hearts would be to take it in, and He so longed that we should really believe that His name is the power in which every knee should bow, and in which every prayer could be heard, that He did not weary of saying it over and over: *in my name*. Between the wonderful *whatsoever ye shall ask*, and the divine *I will do it*, and *the Father ... will give*, this one phrase is the simple link: *in my name*. Our asking and the Father's giving are to be equally in the name of Jesus Christ. Everything in prayer depends upon our apprehending this – *in my name*.[1]

In a Sunday morning sermon, Fr. Jose Poch, the rector of the church I belong to, said "Whenever we pray in the name of Jesus, He says to the Father, 'That's one of mine.'"[2] Jesus' name is the password to the Father.

According to Andrew Murray, to pray in the name

of Jesus means that:

> The name of God is meant to express His whole divine nature and glory. And so the name of Jesus Christ means His whole nature, His person and work, His disposition and Spirit. To ask in the name of Jesus Christ is to pray in union with Him.[3]

Once again:

> His name is Himself, in all His perfection and power. He is the living Christ, and will make His name a power in you. Fear not to plead the name; His promise is a threefold cord that cannot be broken: *And whatever ye shall ask the Father –* **in my name** *– that will I do* (emphasis added).[4]

Above all, to pray in the name of Jesus is to pray with authority. We need the authority of Christ when we are involved in any kind of spiritual warfare. As an example, in my counseling practice I sometimes have a client who has a background of or is involved in occult practices. One such person began to get into them while she was talking to me. Quietly to myself, I claimed by the blood of Christ in Jesus' name the departure of any evil influences. She stopped her prediction relating to me. "It's stopped; I can no longer get the message," she suddenly exclaimed. Once again she tried and was stopped in the same way. She then gave up trying to get the message for the rest of the session. She never tried again.

After she left, I prayed by the blood and power of Jesus Christ, and in His name, over the room. It felt good again. Shortly after, a teenage boy walked in for his appointment. He drew a deep breath and exclaimed: "What do you do with this room? Sprinkle angel dust? It feels so good!" I felt reassured about how I had handled the situation: in the name of Jesus. That is one aspect of praying in the power of Jesus and His name. It defeats the power of Satan. No other power can. That is one way we pray "combatingly" or "wrestle in prayer."

Too often we go into automatic mode when we repeat a behavior. Such can be true when we routinely end our prayers with the words "in Jesus' name." Because of that potential it is important to remember the place faith has in this process, even a tiny amount of faith as mentioned in Matthew 17:20 where the level of faith required to move the proverbial mountain is said to be as small as a mustard seed.

Charles Spurgeon explains the place of faith in praying in Jesus' name. With reference to the lame man who was healed in front of the temple, Spurgeon says:

Let me read the text to you again, that you may see how very remarkably the name of Christ and faith are mixed up. They both occur twice in the verse. What was it that wrought the miracle? Was it the name of Christ, or was it faith in that name? Listen: "His name through faith in His name hath made this man strong, whom ye see and know." And then it is added, "Yea, the faith which is by Him hath given him this perfect soundness in the presence of you all," as if to put the crown on the head of faith rather than on the name of Christ, for faith is sure never to steal that crown. Faith always crowns Christ and, therefore, Christ crowns faith. "Thy faith hath saved thee," said Christ to the woman that was a sinner. "No," says someone, "it was Christ who saved her." That also is true; but Christ said that it was her faith that saved her, and He knew. So, here, it was the name of Christ that wrought the miracle, but it was wrought through faith in that name.[5]

After I became more aware of the power of that name I began to feel a new strength as I prayed and an awe of that precious name, a worship of the One to Whom the name belongs, Jesus of Nazareth.

As we pray in the name of Jesus we also declare to the world our faith. In the first few chapters of Acts there are a number of references to prayer in the name of Jesus. It is a repeated teaching throughout the New Testament. In chapter three of Acts, however, it comes through with a unique emphasis. A man who was lame from birth, has never walked, is laid down every day by the temple. As Peter and John come by, the man asks them for money. After telling the man that he has no money, Peter tells him he can give him something else. Peter says: "I command you in the name of Jesus Christ of Nazareth, walk!" Then Peter pulled him up on his feet. As he did this, the man's feet and ankle bones were healed, so that he leaped to his feet as he came up. Those feet had never been functional before. This made the miracle even greater. All this in the name of Jesus Christ of Nazareth, a lowly town yet the home of the anointed Messiah. This would be too much for the Jewish leaders to handle. And the proof of the validity of what had been said was right in front of them. The man who had been healed in Jesus' name stood there and walked. Yet the Jewish leaders had rejected this Messiah, even killed Him. Now they were proven wrong by the power of His name.

Peter went on to preach a powerful sermon, again reiterating the details of the miracle which been done in Jesus' name. Defeated, all the Jewish leaders could ultimately do was to try to intimidate Peter and John into silence, hoping that by so doing they could suppress the reality of Jesus of Nazareth as the much prophesied Messiah.

In his book *The Name*, Franklin Graham describes the impact of praying in the name of Christ in a more modern-day setting. It was a cold winter day in Washington, DC, when George W. Bush was to be inaugurated as President of the United States. Billy Graham was the natural choice to give the inaugural prayer. But the ceremony was to be held outside and Billy Graham's doctors warned against his exposure to the cold. Yet Graham's relationship with the President Elect had been one of friendship. As a result, the responsibility to offer the inaugural prayer fell on Billy's son Franklin.

The issue arose as to whether he should pray "in Jesus' name," or in the name of God, a term many Christian leaders had used in order to avoid offending some who would be present. To Franklin the issue caused initial conflict. Ultimately, the decision was made because the One over whom this controversy arose was most important: JESUS! As Franklin put it, "I want to please my Father in Heaven no matter the cost." When he delivered the prayer he closed with:

> We pray this in the name of the Father,
> And of the Son, the Lord Jesus Christ,
> And of the Holy Spirit. Amen."

There were amens and applause from the audience.

It was only after Franklin arrived home in North Carolina that the criticism came in from a variety of people against his praying in the name of Jesus. Jews, Muslims and others felt that it had been making the United States look like a Christian nation. Actually, what kind of nation would they call it since it had been founded by Christians and there are references to the Christian God and Christian principles throughout our documents?

For any generation Spurgeon sums up well what it means to have a password to God; to have clear cut access to the Almighty:

> … the name of Jesus is indeed mighty, for it has power with God himself. Hence it is that we never pray without using that blessed name, that is to say, if we are wise. We love to feel all through our prayer and to say when it is ended, "In the name of Jesus Christ our Lord." The keys of Heaven are in the hands of that man who knows how to use aright the name of Jesus.[6]

TWELVE

A Porch to the Father's Home

Most of us have probably had experiences where we felt sheer panic, and then there was God! When I was a student at UCLA, I worked in the main library. At that time the library had a ground-level floor, and below that were a number of descending underground levels. These were accessed by steep stairs. Above each level was a wire see-through gate that was locked each night. If someone wanted a book from these various levels, they put the request in a chute and sent it down to the proper level. The person working at that level would find the book, put it in the chute, and send it back up. The books most unlikely to be requested were housed on the bottom two levels and were therefore worked by only one person. Because I was unfamiliar with the physical setting of the various more active levels, and fewer demands were made of those lower levels, the bottom two were my assignment on my first day at work.

At first it seemed ideal. Almost no one wanted any books from me, so I was literally being paid to study. When evening came my job was simple: on the bottom floor turn off each of the light switches which were located at the end of certain book stacks. Then go up the stairs to the next level, lock the gate at the top of the stairs, and turn off those lights. Keep in mind that this whole process, simple as it seems, took some time for a newcomer who didn't know where anything was. In addition to that complication, I was covering two floors which had to be closed down, not one like everyone else.

On my first day of work, however, after I had shut down my two bottom floors and it was time to close the library itself, I started up the stairs from the bottom level to the next level and then glanced up at the gate at the top of the stairs. I gasped in horror. My stomach clutched. The gate was locked already, as were all the gates above it, and beyond all the gates was pitch black darkness. The whole, huge library had emptied out. I was alone, twelve floors below street level. No one would hear me, no matter how loudly I cried out. Sheer panic swept over me. "Please God, rescue me," I prayed.

Then suddenly I heard a noise above me, followed by an age-long silence. Then I heard it again, and a light went on several floors above me. Someone was there. I shouted and rattled the gate. Someone had come back because he had forgotten his keys. My nightmare was over.

Just chance? I don't think so. Once again God had intervened, this time in a very different way than before in Mexico. But the end result was the same, comfort. God doesn't always say "Yes" to our prayers. Sometimes He says "Yes," sometimes He says "No," and sometimes, "Wait." But He always hears us and does what we ourselves would do if we were God.

As an old Bible teacher used to say, "God is no man's debtor." God never fails. But He can at times be unpredictable. I have found in my own life that God never fails, but He often changes His methods. He may use different people, techniques and timing to come to our rescue so that we never depend on the method instead of God Himself. In II Corinthians 12:9 He promises: "My grace is sufficient for thee; for My strength is made perfect in weakness."

Life's problems change and so do God's methods of helping and comforting us. My friend was wrong in her drunken behavior, but God used that small space of time with Ed as a comfort and a place of safety for me. Later on, that night in Mexico became a treasured memory when I had to choose to give Ed up because of our conflict spiritually. That was not God's usual way of comfort after a broken relationship. Nor does He always rescue us from locked buildings.

Bad things sometimes happen, even to Christians. At the time of the writing of this book, Christians are being beheaded or crucified, executed with a denial of Christ offered as the only way of escape. Has God abandoned these Christians? No, because He has promised never to leave us or forsake us. He has never promised a life of ease, but who of us knows the comfort which is given to these brave martyrs in their greatest hour of need. Perhaps visions which transcend all that is around them. Perhaps pain relief from the loving hands of the Great Physician Himself.

A few days ago, my granddaughter shared with me a quote from George MacDonald which offers a comforting view of the joy and sorrows of this world we live in.

> This world if it were alone, would not be worth much – I should be miserable already; but it is the porch to the Father's home, and He does not expect us to be quite happy, and knows that we must sometimes be very unhappy, till we get there.

I shared this with a young man who is trying to find his own way in this world. He pulled out his cell phone and copied the quotation, commenting that he too liked porches, a place to let down and contemplate. That started my own contemplation on the subject.

Porches are very close to the house they belong to. But they are definitely not IN the house. A porch is a lovely place at the end of a balmy spring day. With cool breezes gently blowing and trees swaying in the wind, life feels good again. Sometimes when life doesn't feel so good, on the porch at the end of a day, alone with nature or with an understanding friend, there is a safe feeling of being close to the Father's house. This earth would feel frightening indeed if it were far from the Father's House. Knowing that this earth is just the porch of Heaven makes earth less scary and Heaven that much less distant and strange.

Yet, just like life itself, porches are inconsistent places. They are not immune from dust storms or falling rain or snow. Wild animals can run across a porch, as can strangers. Porches cannot shield from hurricanes, tornadoes, or earthquakes. But they are lovely places for hanging plants, rocking chairs, and a cup of hot tea.

As those who know Christ as Saviour, we already know that Heaven is to be our eternal Home with Him. And it feels safe to know that on the porch of earthly life, while we enjoy that which God has given us on this earth, and suffer its pangs as well, we live in the safety of the shadow of our eternal home. We live on the porch of Heaven.

As I go out sometimes and stand on the balcony with the mountains showing in the distance, I have sometimes looked at the sky and felt its vastness. "Where is Heaven?" I would think. "It looks so far away." But as I realize that the actual moment of passing from earthly life to the porch of God's home is immediate, my anxiety leaves.

There are events on earth which are far more

frightening than my balcony experience, and many smaller ones too, but knowing that we have that porch which immediately leads to Home can be a comfort. Someday the pain will not reach us, and meanwhile we have a God-given appointment to perform our task for God on this earth. Nor will the actual transition from earth to Heaven be slow. It will be in the "twinkling of an eye." (I Corinthians 15:52) As Christ was dying on the cross, that immediacy was shown in His words to one of the thieves on the cross next to Him. "Today shalt thou be with me in paradise." (Luke 23:43) Today! Not tomorrow. No mention of what we call "soul sleeping."

In II Corinthians 5:18, we read that when we are absent from the body, we are at that moment present with the Lord. When that heart stops beating, you are at Home with God. You are off the porch and in God's Home, safe! There is no long flight through the darkness.

In Psalm 23 the journey referred to as the valley of the shadow of death means the process on this earth which leads to our eternal Home. The porch of earth becomes the porch of Heaven as we arrive. The porch of Heaven is right next to and connected with the eternal mansion of God, close by and kept from us by a simple heartbeat.

In one of Charles Spurgeon's volumes on the Psalms, he quotes a remarkable summary from

Alexander Maclaren of the imagery to be found in Psalm 23:

> "I will dwell in the house of the Lord for ever." This should be at once the crown of all our hopes for the future, and the one great lesson taught us by all the vicissitudes of life. The sorrows and the joys, the journeying and the rest, the temporary repose and the frequent struggles, all these should make us sure that there is an end which will interpret them all, to which they all point, for which they all prepare. We get the table in the wilderness here. It is as when the son of some great king comes back from foreign soil to his father's dominions, and is welcomed at every stage in his journey to the capital with pomp of festival and messengers from the throne, until at last he enters his palace home, where the travel-stained robe is laid aside, and he sits down with his father at his table.[1]

In this quotation we see both the process and the end result, life on this earth ending for most of us in a period of going toward the Father's house, living on the Porch, until in one moment we reach Home.

I have repeated memories from when I was a small child of my father getting up in Wednesday night prayer meeting to just share the 23rd Psalm. It seemed to be an anchor in his life. On his deathbed his last known words referred once again to Psalm 23. The God Who had brought him this far would bring him Home.

It is easy to forget Hebrews 12:1. "Wherefore seeing we also are compassed about with so great a cloud of witnesses, let us lay aside every weight, and the sin which doth so easily beset us, and let us run with patience the race that is set before us ..." Many of us are skeptical when there is allegedly visual contact with one or more of these witnesses. Yet they are more than just a comfort to a small few. They are evidence of the eternal destiny of those who belong to God through Jesus Christ. Great saints have often validated these stories by their own experiences.

As he was entering the process of dying, D. L. Moody, one of the great preachers of the 19th Century, looked forward to seeing his Lord:

> "Some day you will read in the papers that Moody is dead," he had said at New York on a hot Sunday in August, 1899. "Don't you believe a word of it. At that moment I shall be more alive than I am now. ... I was born of the flesh in 1837, I was born of the Spirit in 1856. 'That which is born of the flesh may die. That which is born of the Spirit shall live for ever.'" ... Moody wrote in pencil in his usual bold hand, barely

palsied by weakness: "To see his star is good but to see his face is better."

As the next winter dawn broke, Friday, December 22nd, 1899, Moody stirred from an hour's deep sleep that had ended a fitful night of increasing weakness.

Suddenly Will [his son] heard "in slow measure words": "Earth recedes, heaven opens before me!" Will hurried across.

"No, this is no dream, Will. It is beautiful. It is like a trance. If this is death it is sweet. God is calling me and I must go. Don't call me back!"

At that moment Mrs. Moody entered.

"Here is Mother, Father!"

Moody said "rather faintly but clearly 'Mama, you have been a good dear wife,'" and began to slip into unconsciousness, murmuring, "No pain, no valley, it's bliss."

… "Then he said, '… I went to the gate of heaven. Why, it is so wonderful, and I saw the children!'

"Will said, 'Oh, Father did you see them?'

"And he said, 'Yes, I saw Irene and Dwight,' and then when Will cried, he said: 'You must not cry, Will, you have work to do.'

"Will said with anguish, 'Oh, if I could only go.'

"But he said, 'No, Will, your work is before

you.'"[2]

In a similar manner, my own mother who was not given to fantasies or emotionalism exhibited a connection with those who had gone before. She had been in a serious car accident and was slowly dying. When my daughter and I visited her in the hospital the night before she died, she told us that her mother and father and one of her sisters, who had died long before, had come to visit her. Her face was joyous and her spirit uplifted.

Many people who have experienced these evidences of seeing something related to Heaven are reputed to be quite stable individuals. My parents were both solid Swedes who are known as a group to be slow to become emotional. There are always exceptions, of course, and there are perfectly stable people who under the influence of drugs being used for their physical ailment could have trouble with something like visual distortions. But we do deal with the almighty God of the universe who is perfectly able to do more than even giving us a glimpse of loved one. Hopefully, we remain conscious but at the same time are prayerfully open to such manifestations of God's love and comfort.

And let us not forget Hebrews 12:1: "Wherefore seeing we also are compassed about with so great a cloud of witnesses, let us lay aside every weight, and the sin which doth so easily beset us, and let us run with patience the race that is set before us." They who are already there, and who have taken the very same journey from earth to Heaven, cheer us on and welcome us Home.

If one believes in an eternity with God, one might well ask, "What would I do in my life if I knew I was going to die at a specific time in the near future?" Spurgeon gives us two clear examples. Of Wesley he wrote:

> Let us imitate Mr. Wesley's calm anticipation of his end. A lady once asked Mr. Wesley, "Suppose that you knew you were to die at twelve o'clock to-morrow night, how would you spend the intervening time?" "How, madam?" he replied, "why just as I intend to spend it now. I should preach this evening at Gloucester, and again at five to-morrow morning; after that I should ride to Tewkesbury, preach in the afternoon, and meet the society in the evening. I should then repair to friend Martin's house, who expects to entertain me; converse and pray with the family as usual; retire to my room at ten o'clock; commend myself to my heavenly Father, lie down to rest, and wake up in glory."
>
> Live in such a way that any day would make a suitable topstone for life. Live so that you need not change your mode of living, even

if your sudden departure were immediately predicted to you.[3]

Then of Whitefield he commented:

It was said of Mr. Whitefield, that he never went to bed at night, leaving even a pair of gloves out of its place; he used to say that he would like to have everything ready in case he might be taken away. I think I see that good man standing, with a bedroom candle in his hand, at the top of the staircase, preaching Christ the last night of his life to the people sitting on the stairs; and then going inside the room, and commending himself to God; and going straight away to heaven. That is the way to die; but if you do not live like Wesley and Whitefield lived, you cannot die like Wesley and Whitefield died. May God grant us grace that we may be perfectly ready to die when the time for our departure is at hand![4]

Once again, the changes in how we live, technologically as well as other ways, have been more profound in the last hundred years than in any other span of history before. Furthermore, we have no reason to think that the same rapidity of change will not continue in the future, perhaps until our Lord's return. More than ever, it's that cup of coffee with God that will be at the core of our relationship with God and ultimately will stabilize us through life until we cross that porch to God's mansion. That is what Christ meant when He said that He was leaving this earth to prepare a mansion for us. That He is doing now, as we read these pages. On a much greater scale I suspect that there is a similarity between that and our own preparation for weekend guests, except that Heaven is to be our permanent Home. Exactly how that works is something we will know when we cross over to our heavenly mansion and come face to face with Christ our Saviour.

> Your goodness and unfailing kindness shall be with me all of my life, and afterwards I will live with you forever in your home. – Psalms 23:6 (*TLB*)

When gently from my tight, clenched hands
God took of earthly things which I held dear,
Confused, His love I did not understand;
I grasped still more, lest more should disappear.

But yet in love He took until to Him alone
I turned, for all else seemed
Unsteady, apt to fade; reluctant, still
I gave to Him the things I precious deemed.

He took, but then He gladly gave first of Himself,
His love, His joy, and rest;
Until it seemed the things which I had saved
Were worthless toys compared to heaven's best.

Then, while with willing, open hands
I held all earthly gifts for Him to see
And take or give, apart from my demands,
He gave me back the things He took from me.
                                    – Elizabeth R. Skoglund

Notes

Chapter One

1. Minnie Louise Haskins, *God Knows*. Quoted by King George VI in a Christmas broadcast, 25 December 1939, *Oxford Dictionary of Quotations* (Oxford Press, 1953).

Chapter Six

1. W. Y. Fullerton, D.D., *F. B. Meyer, A Biography* (London: Marshall, Morgan and Scott Ltd., n.d.), 182-183.
2. Ibid.
3. Dwight L. Moody, *Prevailing Prayer* (Chicago: Moody Press, n.d.), 90-91.

Chapter Seven

1. Robert Browning, "Rabbi Ben Ezra," in *Poems of Robert Browning*, ed. Donald Smalley (Boston: Houghton Mifflin, 1956), 287.
2. Ibid., 282.

Chapter Eight

1. Catherine Marshall, *Beyond Our Selves* (New York: Avon Books, 1968), 162-164.

Chapter Eleven

1. Andrew Murray, *The Ministry of Intercession: A Plea for More Prayer* (Aneko Press, 2016. Adapted from the third edition of *The Ministry of Intercession*, originally published by James Nisbet & Co. Limited), 87.

2. Father Jose Poch, "I Believe in Jesus, Part 2," sermon delivered on Aug. 19, 2018, Saint David's Anglican Church, Burbank, CA. (https://youtu.be/ewCXrE_iX2E)

3. Murray, 88.

4. Ibid., 97.

5. C. H. Spurgeon, *The Metropolitan Tabernacle Pulpit* 44 (1898), 500.

6. Ibid., 497.

Chapter Twelve

1. Alexander Maclaren, as quoted by Charles H. Spurgeon, *The Treasury of David*, Vol. 1a (Grand Rapids, MI: Zondervan, 1976), 372.

2. John C. Pollock, *Moody: A biographical portrait of the pacesetter in modern mass evangelism.* (Grand Rapids, MI: Zondervan, 1967), 316-317.

3. C. H. Spurgeon, The Metropolitan Tabernacle Pulpit 32 (1886), 538.

4. C. H. Spurgeon, The Metropolitan Tabernacle Pulpit 38 (1892), 584.

About the Author

A former high school teacher and school counselor, Elizabeth Ruth Skoglund, M.A., LMFT, is a Licensed Marriage and Family Therapist in private practice in Southern California. She is a certified bereavement facilitator for both adults and children. She is the author of more than 50 books and numerous magazine articles, at one time wrote a weekly newspaper column, and has appeared on many TV and radio talk shows. She has been named the Outstanding Scandinavian American 2006-2007 by the American Scandinavian Foundation of Thousand Oaks and was awarded Beautiful Activist 1973 by the Germaine Monteil Cosmetic Company and the Broadway Department Store. A graduate of UCLA with an MA from Point Loma University, she has been listed in various editions of Marquis *Who's Who in America* and *Who's Who in Medicine and Health Care*.

Skoglund's books include: *Life on the Line*; *Bright Days, Dark Nights*; *Amma*; and, more recently, *Found Faithful*; *Divine Recycling*; *More Precious Than a Sparrow*; *I'll Feel Better in the Morning*; and *Finishing Well*. In addition to print books, *Bright Days, Dark Nights* and *Burnout*, as well as *Divine Recycling* and *Life on the Line*, can be found on Kindle.

Skoglund's website is www.elizabethskoglund.com. She can be found on Twitter, Facebook and LinkedIn.

www.ingramcontent.com/pod-product-compliance
Lightning Source LLC
LaVergne TN
LVHW011333080426
835513LV00006B/323